SHAKESPEARE
AND THE CONFINES OF ART

PHILIP EDWARDS

SHAKESPEARE

and the Confines of Art

'No, they cannot touch me for coining;
I am the King himself'

METHUEN & CO LTD
11 New Fetter Lane London E C 4

First published 1968
© *1968 Philip Edwards*
Printed in Great Britain
by Butler & Tanner Ltd
Frome and London

Distributed in the USA
by Barnes and Noble, Inc.

Contents

1 The Contrary Valuations   *page* 1

2 The Sonnets to the Dark Woman   17

3 *Love's Labour's Lost*   33

4 The Abandon'd Cave   49

5 *Romeo and Juliet*   71

6 *Hamlet*   83

7 The Problem Plays (i)   95

8 The Problem Plays (ii)   109

9 The Jacobean Tragedies   121

10 Last Plays   139

   Conclusion   161

   Notes   163

   Index   168

Line references from Shakespeare's plays are from
the New Arden editions. For plays not yet published
in that series, the Globe edition has been used.

I

The Contrary Valuations

If he outlived his Greek campaign, Byron said, he would write two poems on the subject: one an epic, the other a burlesque.[1] We all understand him, because we all have the same double valuation of everything we live through. A war, a family, an institution: work, play or sex; almost at the same moment, they mean everything and they mean very little. Things that are important and firm suddenly seem ridiculous and useless. He is a lucky man who keeps a working balance between his epic and his burlesque visions.

Our views of art, whether of art as a whole, or of individual poems and paintings, share this unstable focus. Every man has something in him which insists that it is all nonsense, but there is another voice, just as insistent, saying that there is nothing in the world which can satisfy a man as this nonsense does.

The two views of art, one of faith and the other of doubt, were summed up in Shakespeare's lifetime by Sidney and Bacon. In the well-known passage in the *Apologie* in which he answers Plato out of Plato's mouth, Sidney claims that, set in the brazen world of nature, the poet has power to deliver a golden world, a world at least as real as nature's world, and truer. 'With the force of a divine breath, he bringeth things forth far surpassing her doings.' Man's wit at its highest point, and that is at the poetic point, is to be more than favourably compared with Nature as a creator (with Nature in a fallen world, it is understood), for the imaginings of the poet have commerce with God, and they 'know what perfection is'.[2]

In *The Advancement of Learning*, and more explicitly in *De*

Augmentis Scientiarum,[3] Bacon seems to agree with all Sidney's assumptions. The world of nature is a fallen world, the soul has desires which things-as-they-are cannot fulfil, and poetry ministers to these divine longings of the soul. But Bacon is much more contented with his habitation in the brazen world, and he is very, very doubtful that the improvement on nature which poetry provides is indeed a 'participation in divineness'. There is a sceptical ring to all he says about the poetic imagination, in spite of his great respect and enthusiasm for the ancient myths, or Poesy Parabolical. Poetry is 'feigned history', its use is 'to give some shadow of satisfaction to the mind of man in those points wherein the nature of things doth deny it'. The spirit of man wants 'a more ample greatness, a more exact goodness, and a more absolute variety, than can be found in the nature of things.' Poetry 'was ever thought to have some participation of divineness, because it doth raise and erect the mind, by submitting the shews of things to the desires of the mind; whereas reason doth buckle and bow the mind unto the nature of things'.

The fine images of this famous sentence leave us in little doubt where Bacon's sympathies lie. Poetry is feigning; it is an activity encouraged by the dissatisfaction of man with things as they are; it twists nature into the forms that appeal to us. The activity of reason in holding man down to 'reality' is clearly for Bacon a much more responsible work than the activity of the poetic imagination. Poetry, he tells us later, 'is rather a pleasure or play of imagination, than a work or duty thereof'. The contempt for wishful thinking which informs Bacon's discussion of Idols lies behind his discussion of poetry ('The human understanding is of its own nature prone to suppose the existence of more order and regularity in the world than it finds'). Granting the poet's skill 'for the expressing of affections, passions, corruptions, and customs', he closes the discussion in *The Advancement* with: 'But it is not good to stay too long in the theatre.'[4]

Art as the creation of truth; art as a distortion of truth to please dissatisfied humanity: these are the 'epic' and the 'burlesque' views. In Shakespeare's plays, most of the remarks about the nature of poetry are uncomplimentary and tend to the burlesque view, in spite of that affirmation about holding, as 'twere, the mirror up to nature, which Wilde believed was spoken by Hamlet 'in order to convince the bystanders of his absolute insanity'. Audrey tells Touchstone 'I do not know what "poetical" is. Is it honest in deed and word? Is it a true thing?' And Touchstone replies: 'No, truly: for the truest poetry is the most feigning.' The hard-headed Theseus links the imagination of the poet, bodying forth the forms of things unknown, with the delusions of lovers and lunatics. Just how far Shakespeare himself shared in the scepticism of his characters, it is the purpose of this book to inquire, but he would hardly have been human had he not, on one and the same day, had faith in his art and scoffed at it too.

Though thinkers divide on the value of art, there seems to be less disagreement about the power of art, or about the human craving for it. Plato would not have dismissed the poets from his republic had he not known how profound and wide the influence of poetry was on the individual and on the group. To think of art as a danger is at least to give credit to its power, as Tolstoy's *What is Art?* shows also. When it comes to the satisfaction which art gives to mankind, those who have faith in art as a means of knowing unite with those who think it fundamentally mendacious.

Is it possible to try to define this satisfaction briefly? There would seem to be a kind of dark lake, which we are all afraid of falling into; the lake of unorganized experience, in which the only certain thing is eventual extinction. The fear is twofold: the fear of confusion, and the fear of time. An instinct of self-preservation makes us recoil against a recognition of our existence as a litter of unrelated happenings jostling into our consciousness, as a complex of experience without regularity or shape, and with no direction except the direction of growing old and growing tired. We turn automatically, like a compass-needle, to whatever has power to gather up the scattered fragments and to impose form on the formless, to reduce anarchy into order, or suggest meaning and direction.

We are all the time selecting from and simplifying the complex of experience and turning it into convenient patterns: if we cannot see that we are doing it ourselves, we can listen to the man next door putting himself in a good light as he recounts some incident he was concerned in. Art, surely, is the high refinement of the shape-making activity which we are engaged in almost every moment of our lives. ('Poetry is a response to the daily necessity of getting the world right,' Wallace Stevens said.[5])

It is perhaps an odd characteristic of the human race that we should want to listen to stories about imaginary people, to hang on our walls crude representations of the visible world, or to sing song-cycles about the distant beloved. But there is no doubt about the intensity of our need to have by our side models or toys which resemble or refer to things which we know and experience in our daily activities. The prehistoric hunter wanted a painting of the hunt in his cave, with the bison struck by the spear between the shoulder-blades; Charles II wanted a life-size nude portrait of Nell Gwynn in his private rooms; the priest wants on his altar a little replica of the cross on which the divine man hung; the Elizabethans wanted to see the death of Richard III performed by actors on a public stage.

Every model, its shape dictated by the nature of the medium (stone, canvas, stage, sonnet), is a simplification of the thing represented. The person or situation represented is of infinite complexity: the mind cannot comprehend its wholeness. The model has its own complexity, no doubt, but it is finite, and its wholeness is at least accessible. In this relative simplicity of the finite model, there is pattern and organization. As Nell Gwynn and the bison are frozen into paint, they are declared: held, and declared. The great exposition which Joyce gave to Stephen Dedalus about the wholeness, harmony and radiance of the literary work seems to me the definitive summing up of the doctrine of art which he properly calls 'epiphany', a manifestation or showing forth.[6] To possess the model is to possess not only a declaration but an assurance, for the model is insisting on its control of what is, in our experiential world, uncontrollable. To suggest that the reason why men turn so eagerly from the thing itself to an ikon or a myth, from the disordered manifold to the articulated representation, is their need for assurance and consolation may seem to put us in the class of savages who believe in therapeutic magic. In *The Principles of Art*, R. G. Collingwood gave an excellent description of the way magical art works, but he was indignant at the idea that art in its high and pure reaches should be confused with emotional therapy.[7] Yet, to alleviate the fear of confusion and allay the fear of time does not seem a shameful function for the very highest art, whatever else it may have to do besides.

In the theatre, for both actors and audience, the physical enactment of the story makes the passage of the drama a vicarious existence: it is something 'lived through'. It is indeed a 'play': a simulacrum of life that is momentarily put in place of life itself. This imitation of life has the beginning and the middle and the end that life itself lacks: the clearly visible sequence of events, the suggestion of proper cause and effect. Whether it is comedy or tragedy, it provides a connected language for what affects people most deeply. It is the property of drama that to participate in its life is to be charged with its power for a long time after one has left the theatre – if the play is any good. It provides a formula to translate our own experience into significance: it acts as a talisman to ward off evil and encourage hope.

Usurpation or the exchange of power is a theme which brings together plays of Shakespeare belonging to quite different genres.[8] One can find it clearly enough in, for example, *Richard II*, *Henry IV*, *As You Like It*, *Othello*, *King Lear*, *Antony and Cleopatra*, *The Tempest*. To lose what one has gained, to be replaced, to grow old and lose one's power – these surely are dominant fears – to be replaced as a lover or a husband, as an owner of goods, as a person of authority, as the strongest member of the family? As husband, father, king, or white man, a person fears his replacement almost as he fears his death, and he hates those who may supersede him. There are big differences in the ways in which different plays of Shakespeare palliate the fear of supersession. Generally speaking, in the comedies the deposed Duke is eventually restored to his lands, and the war of the generations ends in a kind of victory for all. There may be something rather facile about the ending harmony in the middle comedies (I shall argue that Shakespeare thought so), but there is nothing facile about the victory in the last plays – at least not in *The Tempest*. There, the usurped Duke restores his own lapsed power, and arranges the fecundity of children into promise, not threat. The magic *in* the play has a lot to tell us about the magic *of* the play, but that there is a kind of magic in the play's power to soften the shock of the surrender of authority is not to be denied. Critics who consider the last plays to be allegories of reunion and restoration in a happy after-life have certainly fallen under its spell.

In the tragedies, there is not the same restoration of what has been lost, and we see that the consoling patterns of art do not need to take the form of a blithe optimism. To apprehend the way in which plays like *Richard II* and *Antony and Cleopatra* elevate the calamity they so unshirkingly present us with, it is not really necessary to become an anthropologist and invoke spirits like *pharmakos* and *sparagmos*. But I think it is fair to suggest that these stories, as they are acted out before us, have something of the power that older rites had to excite men with the feeling that deprivation, decay and death were part of a grand seasonal necessity. These plays solemnize downfall and usurpation. Partly, these dark things seem, if not reasonable, then explicable. The nameless fear, the isolated shock, the meaningless discontinuity – the things which belong in the dark lake – are taken into the more majestic substance of the tragedy: loss and defeat assume a semi-religious grandeur.

An obvious objection to the notion that art exists in order to console and give assurance is that great literature, when it first appears, causes disturbance and unsettlement rather than tranquillity, and that it generally seems to be the worst kind of art which panders to a craving for comfort. Time and again, what has come to be recognized as great has met fierce resistance, and has had to live through its purgatory of being classed not only by the public but by distinguished critics as obscene, obscure and a denial of art. (As a matter of fact, Shakespeare escaped public resistance: his work was not gradually mediated to the public by the discerning few; popular approval slowly moved him towards acceptance by the critics.) The feeling that April is the cruellest month does not lessen the rejuvenating power of Spring: the conservatism of mankind is no argument against the power of art to help men. Complacency will always have to be broken down before a real work of healing can begin. Great art is sometimes initially rejected by those whom it tries to satisfy. It always takes time to assimilate what is really new, and perhaps familiarity is an important factor in a writer's therapeutic power. And even when it is familiar, a really great work like one of Shakespeare's major tragedies will still unsettle us every time it is played or read. There is, I think, no real incompatibility between disturbance and consolation.

The gap in the consolation theory comes when the writer denies that he has any responsibility for providing a vicarious emotional experience which will enable his audience to see his unorganized experience in patterns convenient to live with. Even this gap can be closed, because a work written to shatter the public's peace can in time become a tame unguent. So far as I can see, however explosive a work was intended to be, if that work endures, it endures because it has the power to become a kind of formula for living – or rather a formula for seeing our own lives. The gap exists, however: art turns against art, proclaims its own dissolution, insists that its function is not to release men from the dark lake but to plunge them into it. The limits of art are decided by the practitioners and by posterity, and not by critical definitions, so there is no point in saying that the defiantly disordered is 'not art'. All the same, there is this to say: the need in man for patterns of order, which some forms of art set out to satisfy, is an incessant and undiminishing need. If people cannot get from major writers the interpretive formulae which they need, they will take them where they can find them, in the stereotypes of cheap writing. To abandon the public to the mercies of meretricious art is not a small responsibility. There is a lot to be said for Sidney's notion of poetry as something which because of its intrinsic delight holds children from play and old men from the chimney corner, and then goes forward to its proper destiny of changing people's lives.

There are raw patches in our lives which the patterns of art cannot mollify. The immediate shock of bereavement makes many people aware how useless the greatest poetry in the world is to bring a sense of order and understanding. But then, as the immediate shock wears off, a bereaved person begins to accept a focusing of his feelings provided by some form of art – sentimental, stoical or religious, as his tastes and knowledge incline.

Even the marriage bed is not free from what Kingsley Amis called 'the life-imitating-art-imitating-life cycle'. Wilde's quip that no one saw London fogs until 'poets and painters ... taught them the mysterious loveliness of such effects' can be taken very seriously.[9] There are a great many points in our lives which we cannot understand and can hardly recognize because art has not accommodated them. One reason for the dislike and distrust of our modern visible environment lies in the decline of representational painting.

It is an elementary fact of physical vision that the brain is always groping after patterns and shapes and that we 'see' objects even if important parts are missing from the retinal image.[10] In our figurative 'vision' of things, too, we are similarly imposing shapes on a tangle of images. What we see seems to depend on the shapes that others have found and taught us – especially artists. It has been claimed that primitive man is simply not aware of events which have not been enshrined in his myths and sanctioned by divine parallel.[11] Art then is, as I understand it, primarily and initially a means of vision, and, necessarily, the vision must in some way content and satisfy us. Human contentment takes strange forms, and almost any ordering and explanation is better than none. It is always to some extent a paradox that tragedy should give a kind of relief.

The perpetual movement of man towards what is coherent and pleasing, Swift called madness. He was aware, if anyone was, of the dark lake, and it was for him not a figment of our fear, but reality; he thought that to try to escape from it was to embrace delusion – 'creaming off nature, leaving the sour and the dregs for philosophy and reason to lap up'.

> If we take an examination of what is generally understood by happiness ... we shall find all its properties and adjuncts will herd under this short definition, that it is a perpetual possession of being well-deceived. ... How fading and insipid do all objects accost us that are not conveyed in the vehicle of delusion! how shrunk is everything as it appears in the glass

of nature! so that if it were not for the assistance of artificial
mediums, false lights, refracted angles, varnish and tinsel,
there would be a mighty level in the felicity and enjoyments
of mortal men.[12]

There is a link between 'the perpetual possession of being well-
deceived' and Bacon's view that the use of poetry was 'to give
some satisfaction to the mind of man in those points wherein the
nature of things doth deny it'. Both Bacon and Swift seem as
confident about 'the nature of things' as they are about the appet-
ency of man to delude himself with comforting fictions. We could
think of the three points of a triangle. One apex is 'unorganized
experience'; the second is the models of reality which art presents;
the third is 'the nature of things'. Bacon claims that, without art,
man can learn the nature of things and it will be different from the
compensatory images of art. Plato will also have an alternative
means of discovering the nature of things and will be free to reject
art as unnecessary or worse. We can hardly find the confidence to
say that the nature of things is what our bleakest moods and
deepest fears suggest it is (Swift?), or that we have a ready way by
reason or observation (Plato, Bacon) to establish the patterns and
laws and the very condition of our existence, and so can dispense
with the structures which art provides as models explaining our
situation.

But, again, we lack confidence in the poets. Their answers are
so various and contradictory for one thing. Or having fastened on
to Dante or Yeats, or Conrad or Shakespeare, with the greatest
enthusiasm, we can't keep it up. We retire to the philosophers, or
to the church, the psychologists or the astronomers. Or we veer
back to the last resort and say that the dark lake of meaningless
contingency is all we know and all we need to know. We stand
in the centre of the triangle, prevented by the 'contrary valuations'
from giving undivided loyalty to art, or reason, or scepticism.

Do our modern myths explain the nature of things, or do they
just soothe us with convenient fictions? The Romantics tell us that
the shape-making activity of man, which is at its most intense
point in art, is a truth-finding activity. Coleridge knew the fear of
the world as a mass of little things, a collection of dead objects.

The 'esemplastic' power of imagination has the power of 're-
ducing multitude into unity of effect' – and all men have imagination; for primarily imagination is the living creativity of all
human perceiving. The poetic or secondary imagination is the
creation of worlds which model the divinely-created world
('nature itself is to a religious observer the art of God') and so
explain to man in a symbolic alphabet the meaning of created
nature ('Art . . . is the mediatress between, and reconciler of,
nature and man').[13]

Coleridge shares Sidney's faith that the poetic imitation of life
is a revelation of the meaning of life, the poet being indeed a
priest of the known God. It needs a very great effort to enter these
regions of belief – but does it not need as great an effort to believe,
at the other extreme, either that Shakespeare's plays only tell us
what we know already (which seems to be the essence of what
Dr Johnson has to say about them), or that they are mere entertainments, giving us a transient pleasure, but of no account when
we turn to the serious business of getting through our lives?

The Shakespeare whom I wish to present is the experimenter,
engaged in a continuous battle, a quarter of a century long, against
his own scepticism about the value of his art as a model of human
experience. All great artists are dissatisfied, and are always trying
again, admittedly: Yeats's alterations of course remind us that
Shakespeare is not unique. But the quality of Shakespeare's dissatisfaction seems to make him a special case. His restless changes
in his forms of drama are something we have to try to explain.
On the one hand, there is the fact of his extraordinary variety.
We can think of the man who in a few years, while he was in his
twenties, created comedies as different in kind as *Comedy of Errors*,
Taming of the Shrew, *Two Gentlemen of Verona* and *Love's Labour's
Lost*, and was at the same time testing the tragic possibilities of the
history-play, of Ovidian horror, and of romantic love. Or we can
just tell off the plays he wrote in two or three years at the turn of
the century: the idyllic or Illyrian comedies, *As You Like It* and
Twelfth Night; the Roman tragedy, *Julius Caesar*; the revenge-
tragedy, *Hamlet*; the bourgeois-farce, *Merry Wives*; the category-

defying *Troilus and Cressida*; the folk-tale tragicomedies, *All's Well* and *Measure for Measure*; and the marital-tragedy, *Othello*. Best of all, we can reflect on the absolute differences between plays of one kind belonging to one period. The protean Shakespeare seems to change his being as he moves from the cosmos of *Hamlet* to that of *Othello*, of *Lear*, *Macbeth*, *Antony and Cleopatra*. Our attempts to synthesize and catch the common factors too often hide the more obvious and more important quality of dissimilarity. The characters speak different languages, were brought up in different moral worlds, face entirely new difficulties – just could not belong in the neighbouring play. In each play a different mind seems to be creating a different world. However great our familiarity with Shakespeare, we cannot overcome the shock of leaving one tragedy and entering the next, and finding that we have to readjust ourselves entirely, take bearings afresh, accustom ourselves to the language, and sink ourselves in the new world of Elsinore, or Venice, or ancient Britain, or Egypt. We just do not have the sense of an exhibition in a gallery by one painter. To think of the consistent weave of the 'world' of the different works of a nineteenth-century novelist – Jane Austen, Dickens, Balzac, Hardy – may be an improper contrast, but I am not sure: for a richness of fictional worlds to compare with Shakespeare's, I think one has to go to the middle-ages or to the nineteenth century, and I find it very hard to think of anyone who changes his sky, air and very ground as Shakespeare does as he moves from one work to his next.

Paradoxically, the miraculous variety of Shakespeare's plays goes hand in hand with a strange kind of reiteration. The gift of his versatility makes his attempts to rewrite the same play all the more remarkable, for we know he doesn't need to repeat himself. It is not so much themes or ideas he repeats as conventions – continuing to turn them inside out to see what new possibilities they reveal. Exploration of conventions is most obvious in comedy: one could argue that there were three separate explorations: of the conventions of 'festive comedy'[14] with its three-stage structure of separation–confusion–harmony, in *Comedy of Errors, Midsummer Night's Dream, As You Like It, Twelfth Night*; of the convention of tragicomic solutions based on folk-tale in *All's Well* and

B

Measure for Measure; of the conventions of romance in his last period, in *Pericles, Winter's Tale, Cymbeline, Tempest*. But *The Tempest* has many points of similarity with *Comedy of Errors*; in each play there is a careful observation of the unities, a strange particularity about the time of day and the location of the action, a shipwreck as cataclysm, a strong use of the idea or the fact of enchantment, the eventual recovery of what has been lost. Recent criticism has drawn attention to Shakespeare's constant preoccupation with romance;[15] the great master's return in his last years to what sometimes seems a childish naïveté of structure in his Romances has always been a critical problem; the commonest image of romance, the shipwreck, is found at the centre not only of *Comedy of Errors* and *The Tempest*, but of *Twelfth Night* and *Pericles*, and forms a vital turning point in the fortunes of the characters in *The Merchant of Venice* and *Othello*. Whatever else Shakespeare's adherence to the unpromising conventions of romance suggests to us, it certainly implies a determination to get something right.

There is considerable difficulty in seeing Shakespeare's experimentation and reiteration as a record of the adjustments and modifications of his opinions about life, or his moods – as the graph of optimism, pessimism, serenity and despair and the rest. The confidence of the philosopher-critics of the nineteenth century in detecting the links between a writer's beliefs and his works is not available to us. But even if it were, we should have to admit, if we were honest, that there is no graph of developing *Weltanschauung* which can make any sense at all: the track of 'bitterness', 'faith', 'hope', 'despair' is a crazy zig-zag. Again, we cannot be so juvenile as to suppose that Shakespeare's 'beliefs' solidified early, and that his experiments are his efforts to embody those beliefs. The theory that Shakespeare was the great ventriloquist,[16] indifferent to what his plays 'meant', who spent his time ringing the changes to please the public is a theory that has the great advantage of lacking pretentiousness and cant, but one cannot honestly survey the evidence, thirty-seven plays, without feeling there was a stricter judge who had to be satisfied: Shakespeare himself. I cannot imagine, on the one hand, that Shakespeare's plays show us his troubles in finding a mythos which could expound his settled or developing theories of what life meant, or, on the other, that the chart of his experimentation is arbitrary, or dependent on external causes.

Let us suppose that Shakespeare recognizes from the first that his office is not to try to find words and forms of drama which will accurately record the manners and doings of men; that, as a dramatist, he knew he was dealing in conventions, the main categories of which (even in those early days of the public theatre in England) were firmly enough established. He was quite prepared to use the established forms of drama and to dispense the kinds of satisfaction inherent in those forms. He knew the shallower and the deeper reasons why men went to the theatre, and he was prepared to meet his part in the contract. He would provide the optimistic narrative of comedy, able to liberate all captives and heal all sunderings; he would provide, in history plays, out of the cruelty and ruthlessness of the Wars of the Roses, a 'myth of origin' for his English hearers, with some pattern of the reasonable emergence of good out of evil; he would provide (though not often), in satire, the discomfiture of the enemies of the subordinate classes; he would give, in tragedy, that solemnity to downfall and death which is supposed to purge us of our own fear.

But as he did all these things, he would (to continue our supposition) for his own satisfaction be trying to enlarge the boundaries of drama and increase the possibilities of tragedy and comedy. The comedies, especially *Love's Labour's Lost* and *Midsummer Night's Dream* are filled with a gentle mockery of the art which builds them. There is something more than good-humoured modesty in this mockery: it appears in very sober form in the later part of *The Tempest*. If we take this mockery seriously, we must apply it to the tragedies as well as to the comedies, unless we are to suppose that because the tragedies deal more openly with pain than the comedies, they are somehow of necessity more genuine and real things. Shakespeare is less easily satisfied than his audiences – or his readers and critics. A comedy may provide that pleasure and contentment which it is the purpose of comedy to give: but it may seem to its author a facile fiction when he thinks of the reality of the difficulties he has allowed his characters to triumph over. The bitterness of a tragedy may be melted by a hint at divine rescue or asylum: yet the intervention may seem a *deus ex machina*. Shakespeare sabotages his own affirmations, and gives to every ringing cry an implausible echo.

The explanation of Shakespeare's experimentation may be that he was trying, within the main forms of tragedy and comedy, to create fictional patterns which could maintain the consoling force of those forms and withstand his own charge that the assurance mediated by his work was cheaply won. In comedy, he would try to celebrate the power of love without belittling the fact of hate. In tragedy, the stubborn realities of malice and lust would be woven into a fabric which satisfies the strongest urge in our blood, the urge towards unity and integration. This is really to say that his efforts take the form of trying to merge comedy and tragedy, or, better, to enclose tragedy within comedy. The pattern of his plays hardly suggests that he ever satisfied himself: the peace of every ending seems to be marred by an ironic note – the author's recognition that it won't do: the note is audible in plays as different as *Twelfth Night*, *Henry V*, *All's Well*, *Antony and Cleopatra*, *The Tempest*.[17]

Shakespeare was not a system-builder: he was an artist, a dealer in dramatic fictions. But I do not see this 'negative capability' which is supposed to accompany his not being a metaphysician. He appears to me to thirst, quite irritably sometimes, after fact and reason. But his only way of 'explaining the universe' was to draw a map, using the conventions of play-making. By adjusting the patterns of art, he would seem to be looking for that fictional ordering which could act as a powerful interpretive formula not only for the experience of his audience, but for his own. To speak too pathetically, it was to lift him above the dark lake, and yet deny nothing that is in the dark lake. So in experiencing and contemplating his own ideal play, the three points of our triangle would come together in a single point: 'unorganized experience', the compensatory models of art, and 'the nature of things'.

He experimented in *Troilus and Cressida* in trying to create a form of art which forbids all the more obvious compensations of order, meaning and hope which inevitably seem implicit in the very structure and plot of more conventional plays. Much more fruitfully, he writes *Othello*, restoring the orthodoxy of tragic order, while still trying to crush the compensations of tragedy into their smallest possible compass. And, at this very time, he is trying to include within the optimistic ordering of comedy the destructiveness and sin which are the theme of the bleakest of the tragedies. In these and all his other experiments, we are not watching Shakespeare come nearer towards or pass further from his own ideas about life. The only way of having 'ideas about life' for a man who lived in his profession as Shakespeare did was to carve out a play, and to see if it would fit. A man obsessed with his own importance and power as an artist might soon – if he had Shakespeare's talent – claim that his plays had answered the problems of life. A man who was too much a prey to the ironic spirit might simply give up. But, for Shakespeare, the pulsing of the contrary valuations of the epic and the burlesque visions seems to – have kept him at it. Nothing but perpetually working at the work that was always inadequate would satisfy him. Nothing would content him but discontent. He was in love with an art that was never immune from his own scepticism about its one-sidedness, its facility. He struggled all his life with the conventions of drama, trying to create out of them a work that was not, to him, patently a fake; he could see it all as counterfeit, yet the Baconian complacency that art was only wishful thinking must have been repulsive to him.

When the mad Lear comes on the stage, fantastically crowned with flowers, he cries, 'No, they cannot touch me for coining; I am the King himself!' This cry seems to me to touch the heart of the 'contrary valuations' in Shakespeare: the sense of guilt that it is all feigning – and yet 'I am the King himself!' – the Sidneian affirmation; even if the poet feels in his heart his coin is counterfeit, he knows too, somewhere, that what *he* issues is the only true currency of the realm.

2

The Sonnets to the Dark Woman

Shakespeare's sonnets to the Dark Woman are a triumph of art built on a persistent demonstration of the weakness of art. What we get from these later sonnets, however, depends on the order in which we read them. A convincing order for the sequence (numbers 127–54) is extremely difficult to establish. Many critics who thought that they could make a pattern out of the sonnets to the young man have given up the task for the dark woman. Dowden wrote: 'I do not here attempt to trace a continuous sequence in the Sonnets addressed to the dark-haired woman . . .; I doubt whether such continuous sequence is to be found in them.'[18] Most readers, in the end, are content to greet the acknowledged great poems as they come: 'My mistress' eyes are nothing like the sun' (130); 'Th' expense of spirit in a waste of shame' (129); 'Two loves I have of comfort and despair' (144); 'Poor soul the centre of my sinful earth' (146). They can claim with reason that the poetry is not suffering in their eyes through the absence of a settled order.

But the belief that there *is* a correct order is hard to subdue. Brents Stirling has made a new attempt, based upon a theory of the way in which the printer might have disarranged the sheets of an ordered collection.[19] In his view, the sequence ends with the great sonnets on lust and on mortification (129 and 146), and three sonnets are independent (128, 138, 145). I shall show why I disagree with such an ending, and why I find the three 'independent' sonnets necessary to the sequence, but first we have to ask what kind of an order we are looking for. We may mean the order in which they were written, an unplanned 'biographical' order. We should then have to ask whether we suppose the sonnets to have been written for and sent to a woman as a liaison progressed or whether we suppose them to be a deliberate record of an affair. The former seems very unlikely. As Auden has reminded us, it is most improbable that the sonnets of the later sequence were ever sent to the woman herself.[20] If you send sonnets to a woman in which you talk of 'the very refuse of thy deeds', and describe her as 'black as hell, as dark as night' and as 'the bay where all men ride', then sooner or later she either refuses to receive the sonnets or refuses to receive the poet. The sonnets themselves show that the intended audience must have been close friends who play a game of overhearing a poet talking to his mistress; it is *they* who are meant to appreciate the pervading irony which the ostensible recipient is supposed not to discern.

Even if we regard the poems as a self-conscious record of a liaison rather than as 'spontaneous' occasional poems sent to a woman, we are still faced with a big difficulty implicit in the search for an autobiographical order. It is unlikely that autobiography will yield order; it is unlikely that a 'real-life' sequence will have the tidiness of a self-explanatory order, with a beginning, middle and end. If we are looking for a history or a diary we may expect it to look as confused as the sonnets now look, left in the order in which they were first printed.

If we turn now to look for a planned sequence, belonging only partly (if at all) to the events of Shakespeare's life, we are at once baulked, as we begin to shuffle the 1609 order, by the interference of our own expectations – the kind of interference which made critics wish to close Sidney's *Astrophil and Stella* with 'Leave me O love which reachest but to dust.'[21] Unless the closest chronological continuity can be established (and it cannot), we can only impose what we wish to find. In a set of sonnets like that which we have before us, we cannot, by re-arranging them, do more than give a personal guess at the pattern of love's progress which we think Shakespeare intended to set out.

All the same, it is my opinion that the Dark Woman sonnets were put forward by Shakespeare as a coherent sequence, a sequence which is as much imaginative as historical, as much thought out as lived out. Although I find it inconceivable that the sonnets were not born out of the deepest personal experience, what Shakespeare gave – to his friends if not to the world – seems to me a very long way from a personal diary. How much revising, re-arranging, new writing was needed in the progress from personal experience no one will ever know, but perhaps Yeats is the poet to think of in analogy.

Where is the sequence to be found? I suggest it is in the order in which the sonnets were first printed in 1609: the order in which they are still printed because no one can find a better. In *The Shakespearean Moment* (1954), Patrick Cruttwell said, 'These sonnets which deal with the lady . . . contain most of the greatness and most of the maturity of the whole sequence; they can be taken as a single poem, in the way in which (for instance) Donne's nineteen *Holy Sonnets* are a single poem.' It is possible to go further than this comparison takes us and argue that the sonnets are a single poem only if they are read in the 1609 order.

There is not very much on the Dark Woman sonnets in the recent studies by E. Hubler, Wilson Knight, C. H. Landry and Murray Krieger. But there are three very stimulating essays in *The Riddle of Shakespeare's Sonnets* (1962) by Northrop Frye, Leslie Fiedler and R. P. Blackmur, all of which in their different ways emphasize the strangeness of Shakespeare's handling of the traditional two faces of Love. These essays, with Cruttwell's chapter, are the best introduction to the problems of the later sonnets.

The first face of love is described in the long sequence of poems to the young man, the second in the appended sequence to the dark woman. The first love is non-physical, a mingling of the two selves or souls into one soul; the second love is a mingling of the bodies of man and woman – will with will – without the marriage of the minds. On the one hand is love without physical intercourse; on the other is lust without spiritual intercourse. Shakespeare makes it clear that love and lust (each directed towards a different person) are intertwined in the lover. The story of the dark woman takes place *within* the narrative of the love for the youth; the fact of lust is included in the history of love. That the two experiences are meant to be seen as simultaneous can be

inferred from the rather forced insertion, at the centre of each
sequence, of the 'triangle' sonnets, 40-2 and 133-4, in which the
poet tells us of the sexual relations between the woman and the
youth. In these sonnets it is clear that the poet is 'in love' with
both the youth and the woman at the same time. They describe
how the woman has deserted his bed for the young man's, they
voice his feeling of being betrayed by both of them, and they
attempt (more or less ironically) various kinds of consolation. The
most profound explanation of the predicament is in sonnet 144.

> Two loves I have, of comfort and despair,
> Which like two spirits do suggest me still:
> The better angel is a man right fair,
> The worser spirit a woman coloured ill.
> To win me soon to hell, my female evil
> Tempteth my better angel from my side,
> And would corrupt my saint to be a devil,
> Wooing his purity with her foul pride.
> And whether that my angel be turned fiend
> Suspect I may, yet not directly tell;
> But being both from me, both to each friend,
> I guess one angel in another's hell.
>   Yet this shall I ne'er know, but live in doubt
>   Till my bad angel fire my good one out.

At one level, the poem expresses by means of puns the fear that
the mistress and the beloved youth are committing fornication and
that the youth will be infected with venereal disease. There is also
the fear that the young man's lust will corrupt him spiritually as
well as physically. If the youth *is* corrupted, then the salvation
offered to the poet in loving him disappears. At another level, the
complicated story of what is happening to three people can be
seen as an image of what is happening to one human soul. The poet
shows himself as a man swinging between salvation and damnation as he obeys the desires of his body and of his spirit. Ultim-
ately, the living-together which the poet describes is the living-
together in his own heart of the purity of love and the impurity
of lust. The final fear is that his own lust will contaminate and
disfigure his capacity to love, and win him soon to hell.

If the two faces of love are to be shown as present at the same time, it has also to be made clear that in essence they are distinct and separate; each kind of affection has its own sequence. It seems right that the lust-sequence should come last. Slowly, after 'all that pain', the sequence of sonnets to the fair youth reaches an equilibrium in the mutual forgiveness of faults when true minds are married (116 and 120 especially). The appending of the second sequence shows how impermanent this equilibrium is, how it is always threatened by the grosser sexual needs. The victory in the first sequence is subdued enough but even so Shakespeare questions it. By adding the Dark Woman sonnets he shows a distrust of the resounding final chord which we shall find again and again in the plays.

The characteristic of the Dark Woman sonnets is that the suggestion of a 'real' relationship is created, running beneath poems which, sometimes ostentatiously, show their failure to crystallize and comprehend this relationship. It is the impression of failure which provides the evidence of the 'real' relationship. It is like defining God by negatives, showing the inability of language to describe Him. We may often enough indulge our fancy about the real relationship which lay behind some love poem and imagine that in life things were not quite as the poet has put it. But love poems do not usually make the effort to hint at a discrepancy; the sense of life is what most of them try to give. I suggest that the most profitable way to read the Dark Woman sonnets is to think of Shakespeare watching his creature-poet at work. The sonnets, strung along a thin line of narrative about wooing, conquest and disgust, are a poet's ordering of his own life, his answering 'the daily necessity of getting the world right'; and Shakespeare is observing his grim failure. As the affair intensifies from courtship to consummation to bitterness, Shakespeare's ironic detachment from his creature becomes less and less, but a distance is maintained throughout.

Each of the first four sonnets is a posture; each introduces a particular kind of artistic ordering which is to be followed up later. Sonnet 127, 'In the old age black was not counted fair', proves that the dark woman is beautiful and is the first of a number of court-ship poems in which the sonneteer, delighting in his own poetic wit, denies the distinction between ugliness and beauty, and hence, by traditional symbolism, denies the distinction between evil and good. The second poem, 'How oft when thou, my music, music play'st', is one of those classed as 'independent' by Professor Stirling. It seems to me the very necessary introduction of the purely conventional wooing-poem. The humble lover watches his mistress at her music, envies the keys which touch her hand and pleads for the gratification of a kiss. To explode this world of sighing poetry-love, there follows the great sonnet on lust (129):

> Th' expense of spirit in a waste of shame
> Is lust in action; and till action lust
> Is perjured, murd'rous, bloody, full of blame,
> Savage, extreme, rude, cruel, not to trust;
> Enjoyed no sooner but despisèd straight;
> Past reason hunted, and no sooner had,
> Past reason hated as a swallowed bait
> On purpose laid to make the taker mad.
> Mad in pursuit, and in possession so;
> Had, having, and in quest to have, extreme;
> A bliss in proof, and proved, a very woe;
> Before, a joy proposed; behind, a dream.
> All this the world well knows; yet none knows well
> To shun the heaven that leads men to this hell.

Magnificent though this sonnet is, taken by itself, it gains a special force from its position. The early sonnets in this sequence, before the reversal in 137, provide a study in self-deception, and the evidence for this is sonnet 129. Here the poet has a momentary vision of himself as a madman, here he sees his courtship as the longings of lust for its reward of self-loathing. Every wooing-poem which follows this is coloured by it; the poet who has had this vision of what he is doing in seeking the favours of the dark woman goes on writing poems which 'convince' him that he is in no danger, poems in which he is able to smother his moral sense in his delight in his own poetic skill. Far from being an ending to the sequence, the sonnet on lust finds its proper place near the beginning. It poses the question to which the sequence as a whole finds that there is no answer; why does a man willingly poison himself?

In the fourth sonnet, 'My mistress' eyes are nothing like the sun', the poet explores the possibilities of the common anti-petrarchan convention.

> My mistress' eyes are nothing like the sun;
> Coral is far more red than her lips' red;
> If snow be white, why then her breasts are dun;
> If hairs be wires, black wires grow on her head.
> I have seen roses damasked, red and white,
> But no such roses see I in her cheeks;
> And in some perfumes is there more delight
> Than in the breath that from my mistress reeks.
> I love to hear her speak, yet well I know
> That music hath a far more pleasing sound;
> I grant I never saw a goddess go:
> My mistress, when she walks, treads on the ground.
>   And yet, by heaven, I think my love as rare
>   As any she belied with false compare.

At first, this sonnet seems to be a direct attempt to cut through the nonsense of 128 and to come to a 'real' relationship. Rejecting idiotic comparisons, it seems a sane and human acceptance of a woman for what she is. The poet's love seems truer and warmer in its independence of poetic flattery. For the reader to see the poem only in this way, however, is to slip into the very trap which Shakespeare wants to show his poet falling into. Who is the woman who is contemplated so humanly, so warmly, so confidently? The Dark Woman, who is shortly to be shown as an agent of damnation. When we read this poem in its proper context, we can see that the final couplet conveys a double impression. First we congratulate the poet on the honesty of his love which needs no lying comparisons to assist it. Then we reflect on the continuous play in these sonnets between fairness–beauty–virtue and darkness–ugliness–vice, and we wonder whether a sophistical confusion between these two poles is not at work here too. Because all women, however beautiful, are 'belied' by being compared with goddesses, are all women equally beautiful and equally worthy of love? The poet has a right to love whom he will, and

to accept a plain woman is no crime, but in so far as the ground
of his acceptance is the equality of women as non-goddesses, he
shows himself insensitive to the distinction (symbol of a moral
distinction) between ugliness and beauty. Shakespeare does not say
outright that the woman is ugly; students are taught that 'reeks'
does not imply halitosis or garlic. But no one can read the poem
without a sense of considerable unattractiveness in the dun breasts,
black hair, pallid cheeks and breath which, if it is not sour, is not
exactly sweet. The sonnet may be seen as a parody of the usual
anti-petrarchan sonnet in which the poet rejects ornamental comparisons because true beauty needs no such aids. While showing
that a woman gains nothing from false flattery the poet implies
that physical demerits (the emblems of spiritual demerits) are of
no account with him. With the gallantry of his wit, he once more
confounds all distinction between women. To understand what
the lover really achieves in this sonnet, we can turn to any of the
later poems, sonnet 150 for example:

> To make me give the lie to my true sight
> And swear that brightness doth not grace the day.

The ugliness of the woman is made obvious in the subtle poem
which follows (131). The poet jokes that in spite of her unpromising face, his mistress must be a conventional beauty because she
tyrannizes over his heart like the heroine of any ordinary sonnet-
sequence. He again denies distinction ('Thy black is fairest in my
judgement's place') and tells us outright, for the first time, of the
woman's viciousness:

> In nothing art thou black save in thy deeds,
> And thence this slander, as I think, proceeds.

What a great joke it is for him to be in love (if that's the word)
with an ugly woman of dubious character and to be able to prove
her as fair as the fairest – and, by means of the proof, insult her.

Sonnet 132 carries the jesting on and deepens the sense of ugliness.
Conventional comparisons, rejected in 130, are trotted out with

an accent which cleverly degrades the woman as they seem to praise her.

> And truly not the morning sun of heaven
> Better becomes the grey cheeks of the east,
> Nor that full star that ushers in the even
> Doth half that glory to the sober west
> As those two mourning eyes become thy face.

The denial in this poem is emphatic, 'Then will I swear beauty herself is black', and the denial is promised as a consequence of her granting him 'pity'. The denial of value is a price he is willing to pay for the satisfaction of his lust.

The 'triangle' sonnets, which follow, are important in reminding us at this stage of the existence of the other kind of love and of the contamination of the higher by the lower kind. The two poems make the woman's 'black deeds' more real as they describe her promiscuity and draw her as a demon whose loathsome magnetism enslaves her victims. The extraordinary 'will' sonnets, 135 and 136, show what wit can do to turn what is dreadful into amusement; the lover's plea for pity is advanced in a crudely physical way. His arguments for being admitted to her favours are at the level of mutual sexual satisfaction; he equates his whole being with his carnal desire and his virility:

> Make but my name thy love, and love that still
> And then thou lovest me, for my name is Will.

He is still laughing at the joke as he unites with the woman he knows the worst of in a congress whose emotional and spiritual consequences he has already foreseen in sonnet 129. The climax of the sequence – the 'kiss' sonnet of discreeter series – is sonnet 137. At the moment of fruition, there is immediate and overpowering revulsion.

> Thou blind fool, Love, what dost thou to mine eyes
> That they behold and see not what they see?
> They know what beauty is, see where it lies,
> Yet what the best is take the worst to be.

If eyes, corrupt by over-partial looks,
Be anchored in the bay where all men ride,
Why of eyes' falsehood hast thou forged hooks
Whereto the judgement of my heart is tied?
Why should my heart think that a several plot
Which my heart knows the wide world's common place?
Or mine eyes seeing this, say this is not,
To put fair truth upon so foul a face?
    In things right true my heart and eye have erred,
    And to this false plague are they now transferred.

The question, why does a man betray himself and swallow the
bait?, continues for the rest of the sequence, but in the end there
is no answer to give beyond the simple statement that it has
happened.

The sequence continues with a series of sonnets written in bed.
The rapid alterations of mood, the contradictions in viewpoint,
may seem bewildering, but they are by no means an indication
that the order is haphazard. The mood as a whole is of restless
conflict in the single attempt to write the poem that makes the
unbearable look bearable. Sonnet 138 ('When my love swears
that she is made of truth / I do believe her though I know she
lies') tries to follow the pattern of conciliation used in the sequence to the young man – not to insult and despise but to
recognize and accept one's own imperfections as well as those of
one's partner. But the resolution has a very hollow sound; they
will lie to each other and each will pretend to believe the other,
for 'love's best habit is in seeming trust'. On this thin surface they
will try to build, but all that they have with which to build is
sexual pleasure:

        Therefore I lie with her and she with me,
        And in our faults by lies we flattered be.

In 139, he shows himself afraid of his own facility for consoling
himself by writing down specious excuses for the woman. The
mood is very similar to the mood of sonnet 35 in which the poet
begins to pour out tired exculpatory analogies on his friend's
behalf, and then pulls himself up in disgust at his own lack of

moral courage. In sonnets 141 and 142, the word 'sin' enters for the first time, and the poet sees his suffering as condign punishment. Orthodox moral judgement of himself and his mistress as adulterers brings a new perspective into the sequence.

Sonnets 143, 144, 145, 146 seem to me to be of central importance. Two of them are very weak, the other two are very powerful. Indeed, in 145 ('Those lips that Love's own hand did make') we have one of the worst of all the sonnets, and in 146 ('Poor soul the centre of my sinful earth') one of the best. But when he is writing badly, Shakespeare does so intentionally, not for the first or the only time (we may think of the sonnets given to the young nobles in *Love's Labour's Lost*). In each of these sonnets, Shakespeare – or rather his poet – tries to make the peculiarly unhappy fact of his predicament conform to a different poetic 'idea'; he tries out different objectifications of the intolerable position he finds himself in – and none of them 'works'. Sonnet 143, a study in whimsical self-derision, turns the lover into a neglected baby crying for the mother who is chasing a hen. If this ludicrous image for deserted lover and predatory female lowers the poet, the poem yet provides in the rounded movement of its own logic the promise of consolation:

> But if thou catch thy hope, turn back to me
> *And play the mother's part*, kiss me, be kind.

The next sonnet in the group is 'Two loves I have of comfort and despair', which we have already discussed. Like the lust-sonnet, it gains extra depth from its position, rudely cancelling out the propositions of a weak preceding sonnet. It is followed in its turn by a remarkable song (145). A characteristic and understandable note on this appears in the Harbage and Bush 'Pelican' edition of the Sonnets: 'The authenticity of this sonnet, in tetrameters and rudimentary diction, has been questioned, with considerable show of reason; in any case, it is not in context with the adjacent sonnets.' The Ingram and Redpath edition says:

> These trivial octosyllabics scarcely deserve reprinting. Some editors have considered the poem spurious on account of its

c

feeble childishness. It would seem arbitrary, however, to rule
out the possibility that one of Shakespeare's trivia should have
found its way into a collection not approved by him.

> Those lips that Love's own hand did make
> Breathed forth the sound that said 'I hate'
> To me that languished for her sake;
> But when she saw my woeful state,
> Straight in her heart did mercy come,
> Chiding that tongue that ever sweet
> Was used in giving gentle doom,
> And taught it thus anew to greet:
> 'I hate' she altered with an end
> That followed it as gentle day
> Doth follow night, who like a fiend
> From heaven to hell is flown away.
>   'I hate' from hate away she threw,
>   And saved my life, saying 'not you'.

It can surely be argued that this absurd song *does* fit the place it
is given. The idea of the woman's hate, as opposed to coldness or
indifference, was first introduced in 142 and is continued here and
in later sonnets. The metaphor of heaven and hell makes a direct
link with the preceding 'two loves' sonnet and with the mortification-sonnet which follows next. I suggest that this despised
poem should be taken as a satirical picture of a poet smoothing
out life's problems, whistling to keep his spirits up. All's well that
ends well; the fiend flies out of the window. The feebleness of the
poem is an exaggerated comment on the weakness of poetry as
a means of arranging one's life or even portraying it. Yet, exaggerated as it is, it does make a comment on poetry as a whole.
It uses a magic which is quite patently ineffectual, but it draws our
attention to poetry as a kind of magic which may or may not
work. The poem which follows is a particularly powerful poem.
Although, as with two earlier poems I have mentioned, it gains
extra force from exploding a namby-pamby predecessor, I believe we must also say that it is coloured by its predecessor.
The mortification-sonnet is akin to the song in being a poet's
attempt to relieve the pressures on his life through the perspective
of art.

Poor soul, the centre of my sinful earth,
[Fooled by] these rebel pow'rs that thee array,
Why dost thou pine within and suffer dearth,
Painting thy outward walls so costly gay?
Why so large cost, having so short a lease,
Dost thou upon thy fading mansion spend?
Shall worms, inheritors of this excess,
Eat up thy charge? Is this thy body's end?
Then, soul, live thou upon thy servant's loss
And let that pine to aggravate thy store;
Buy terms divine in selling hours of dross;
Within be fed, without be rich no more:
    So shalt thou feed on Death, that feeds on men,
    And Death once dead, there's no more dying then.

That mortification of the pride of the flesh and a life turned towards God can be an answer to the attack of the female devil ('there's no more dying then') is ruled out by the next sonnet –

My love is as a fever longing *still*
For that which longer nurseth the disease.

('still' is at least as likely to have here its modern meaning as the older meaning of 'always'.) Death is not dead: 'I desperate now approve / Desire is death.' Sonnet 146 does not put the claims of religion any the less nobly because it does not serve the poet as more than a transient insight into what might be. It may seem a greater poem because of its hint of tragedy in that a man should know what this poem knows and yet be unable to avail himself of what the poem offers. And I certainly do not think that its value is lessened if we see it as one of a series of poems in a *dramatic* sequence in which the hero, a poet, restlessly turns to different poetic images of his own troubles.

The wild music of the few remaining sonnets puts them among the greatest writing of Shakespeare. There is never a last word. The poet accepts his incurable condition as a madness in 147, but then he goes on to degrade himself in anger (149 and 150), blaming *her* for entangling him:

If thy unworthiness raised love in me,
More worthy I to be belov'd of thee.

The obscene sonnet 151 tries vainly to find refuge in the idea that there being nothing nobler in man than his sexual desire, he might find contentment in simply being the woman's drudge. Sonnet 152 ends with yet another repetition of the inexplicable:

> And, to enlighten thee, gave eyes to blindness,
> Or made them swear against the thing they see;
> For I have sworn thee fair; more perjured eye,
> To swear against the truth so foul a lie.

After this, the sequence evaporates in two perfunctory sonnets on the theme of Cupid's brand heating a well.

> Past reason hunted, and no sooner had,
> Past reason hated as a swallowed bait
> On purpose laid to make the taker mad.

The story of the poet and the dark woman is not some isolated adventure. Shakespeare is writing about sexual desire, and he portrays it as a degradation that a man cannot withstand. What is perhaps not improperly called the fear of desire is partly submerged in Shakespeare's earlier plays but it reappears at the turn of the century and in almost every play from *Measure for Measure* onwards there is an acknowledgement of the supposed disjunction between the marriage of minds and the union of bodies. In the last plays there is much that is perplexing on this subject. What we have read in the Sonnets helps to explain the chiaroscuro of Marina in the brothel, Polixenes' vision of childhood innocence and the anxiety of Prospero's spirits to keep Venus out of the wedding masque. Auden was right to conclude his essay on the sonnets with the address to all-enslaving Venus from Shakespeare's last offering, *The Two Noble Kinsmen*.[22]

At the moment what concerns us is not Shakespeare's 'attitude to sex' but his attitude towards art. The drama of the Dark Woman sequence is not alone the drama of the curse of the granted wish, but the drama of the poet groping to materialize his emotions in verse. Shakespeare sets poetry the task of describing a certain kind of hopelessness and he shows poetry pulling like a tidal current away from hopelessness towards resolution of one kind or another. Although individual poems, however brilliant, may be 'failures' in that they are shown to be separated from the life they pretend to record, the cumulative effect of the sequence is success of the highest order, not failure. By accretion and implication, the condition is described. It will be found in some of the earlier comedies that a triumph of art can lie in a partial repudiation of art. Winning a victory by allowing a series of defeats resembles what Eliot was doing in *Four Quartets*, for there too the poetry moves round and about, trying every sort of key and tempo, cancelling out its rhetoric, defying heroics, trying to find the poetry for

> A condition of complete simplicity
> (Costing not less than everything).

Another poet than Shakespeare might have made the lust-sonnet and the mortification-sonnet the culmination of his sequence; at the end of the affair the poet-lover is made to recognize the madness of desire and to turn his back on all earthly things. In his very ingenious and persuasive study, Brents Stirling writes that his hypothesis 'accounts for seemingly random displacement – the appearance of a grim sonnet on lust (129) between the dainty, affected 128 and 130, and the sequential absurdity of a pretty sonnet like 145 followed by the *de profundis* note of 146'. I have tried to show that 129 and 146 have a quite special importance in irrupting into the narrative just where they do in 1609, and in not coming at the end. Shakespeare is dealing with great complexities of the mind and the heart, on to which is added the driving need of the poet to use his art, with all *its* complexities, to make sense of his condition. The course of knowledge will not be a symmetrical graph.

3

Love's Labour's Lost

The dominant rhythm of Shakespearian comedy has been quite admirably described by Northrop Frye in *A Natural Perspective*. Though there is no such thing as a 'typical' Shakespearian comedy, it is clear that in a great many plays the action is in three stages: separation, bewilderment, harmony. Separation, isolation, pain are the condition in which the plays begin; union and happiness are the goals; the characters of comedy are moved from the first stage to the third by means of a period of purgatorial confusion.

This particular pattern of healing is clear in *The Comedy of Errors*. Aegeon has lost his wife and one of his twin sons at sea, the other son has been gone five years on the quest for his missing brother. As the play opens Aegeon is welcoming the death due to him only for being what he is, a Syracusan at Ephesus. The searching brother tells us outright that

> I, to find a mother and a brother
> In quest of them, unhappy, lose myself. (*I, ii, 39–40*)

The bewilderment which follows, through the confusions among two pairs of twins, needs no description. The feeling of enchantment, even to the point of madness, falls strongly upon Antipholus of Syracuse, as his very identity seems to come into question (e.g. II, ii, 212–16; III, ii, 37–43). In the end he and his Dromio make their way with swords drawn out of the bewitched town and escape into the safety of a priory. After a final confusion, the members of the divided family find one another: husband greets wife, parent greets child, brother greets brother;

Antipholus of Syracuse will marry Luciana, and they all retire to a feast. It is a pity that the mother's last words have fallen under a cloud of textual suspicion:[23]

> Go to a gossips' feast, and go with me:
> After so long grief, such nativity.   (*V, i, 405–6*)

The earlier comedies which most clearly show the three-stage action, in which the characters lose their former selves before being brought to their happiness, are *A Midsummer Night's Dream*, *As You Like It* and *Twelfth Night* (though the procedure is not so very different in *Two Gentlemen of Verona* and *Much Ado about Nothing*, even *All's Well that Ends Well* and *Measure for Measure*). In these three plays, as in *Comedy of Errors*, it seems an important point that the characters scarcely earn their deliverance by their own efforts (though they may deserve it). As they are plunged into bewilderment, so, suddenly, are they released from it into the haven which they have been hoping for. The confusions and mistakings in Ephesus, the wood near Athens, the forest of Arden, or Illyria, seem to be more an imposed period of preparation than a certain stage in human contriving. The solid enough world of disappointment or frustration in which the characters start has to be dissolved before there is reintegration in the new life.

Whatever the period of bewilderment may do to the characters, it is clear what it does to the spectators, for the confusions and misunderstandings are a main source of the play's humour. Though comedy is a very different thing from the comic, a comedy needs laughter as an axle needs oil. We are all on the side of comedy, because we all fight against separation and constriction, fight towards relationship and society. But it is easier to accept the triumphs of comedy if we are purged by laughter. C. L. Barber has written a well-known book associating Shakespeare's comedies with the holiday spirit and holiday activities of his audience. The afternoon on which the comedy is played is indeed holiday. The tonic of laughter is the release from the tyranny of the actual. Plays like *Comedy of Errors* and *As You Like It* dissolve our own difficulties and constraints in laughter at a world of fantasy. For the audience as for the persons of the play, the careworn appearance of things melts into the stuff of dreams, and we can be ready to respond to the celebration of concord and near relationship. It is all a dream, but it is the kind of dream that keeps us going.

It has been too much commented on to need more than the mere remark that the region of the 'second stage' of the comedy, is (beginning with *Two Gentlemen of Verona*) more often than not a wild place, removed at any rate from courts and cities. It is very hard to imagine Shakespeare's comedies without the interludes away from the populated places, so central are these interludes in so many of the best works, like *As You Like It* and *The Winter's Tale*. The absence of this interlude in *Much Ado About Nothing* and *Twelfth Night* may account for the striking differences in tone between these plays and their fellows. The wild place is clearly a proper setting for people to lose themselves in order to find themselves, and, as a theatrical image, is a powerful solvent for the audience.

What one would think of as one of the essential constituents of Shakespearian comedy, love between the sexes, finds little place in *Comedy of Errors*. It is useful that we should be reminded that mating is not the only kind of union among people. *Two Gentlemen of Verona* offers us the link of friendship. Shakespeare's most moving unions, in the Romances, are of father and child, friends and long-married couples. Yet the marrying of young people is after all the most vital and impressive union, and sexual love seems the best subject for the play that is to celebrate the successful quest for union. In any case the kind of assurance that the ritual of this kind of comedy is to provide is the assurance of fertility: that is to say, the assurance that sexual desire, not death, nor time, is dominant, that it overcomes what confronts and objects to it, and that it leads to satisfaction and procreation.

> Wedding is great Juno's crown:
> O blessed bond of board and bed!
> 'Tis Hymen peoples every town;
> High wedlock then be honoured.

Honour, high honour and renown,
To Hymen, god of every town!

(As You Like It, V, iv, 147–52)

Honour, riches, marriage-blessing,
Long continuance and increasing,
Hourly joys be still upon you!
Juno sings her blessings on you.

Earth's increase, foison plenty,
Barns and garners never empty,
Vines with clust'ring branches growing,
Plants with goodly burden bowing:
Spring come to you at the farthest
In the very end of harvest!
Scarcity and want shall shun you;
Ceres' blessing so is on you.

(Tempest, IV, i, 106–17)

No winter in Ceres' blessing! Spring is to follow at the end of
harvest for the married lovers of comedy. Shakespeare must show
how the paths of lovers will inevitably converge, and that fertile
spring is the only season of the year that counts.

It seems to be in the sub-plot to *The Taming of the Shrew* that
Shakespeare introduced the theme of sexual love into his comedy.
The story of Lucentio and Bianca comes by way of Gascoigne
from Ariosto's *I Suppositi* (1509). We are so familiar with the chastity of Shakespeare's young lovers, that we perhaps do not see
the importance of the change he made from his source, in which
the originals of Lucentio and Bianca have been sleeping together
for a long time. Shakespeare makes them wait for the marriage
bed at the end of the play. The importance of chastity for Shakespeare is something we shall have to touch on if we are to make
any sense out of *Measure for Measure* and *The Tempest*; his troubled
view of sexual relations, which I have commented on in discussing the Sonnets, seems sometimes to lead him to a rather strained
insistence on pre-marital chastity. But the significance of the
change at the moment, of course, is that the ending of comedy
should not merely be a victory over unsympathetic people, but

the fulfilment of a sought-after union. For the lovers to be united
in secret would, in this kind of comedy, quite destroy the play.
The play has not only to enthrone sexual affection, it has also
to hymn the completion of the mating quest it describes.

To the end of his life, Shakespeare continued to mould and re-
mould the clay of his own kind of romantic comedy, though he
'saw through it' from the beginning. That *Love's Labour's Lost* is
an early play, and *Pericles* and *The Winter's Tale* are late plays is
an oddity. Yet the primitiveness of these mature plays could not
exist if there had not been the sophistication of that early play.
Love's Labour's Lost is the comedy which denies itself and refuses
to behave. The mating quest ends not with triumphant wedding
music, but with a disconsolate group of lovers dismissed to a
wintry twelve-months in hermitage or hospital: the only music
is the mocking note of the cuckoo and the 'merry note' of the
owl. In this play Shakespeare refuses the 'proper' ending: in the
later comedies he insists on the ending above all things, but refuses
the 'proper' contents. The impulse, in his early years, to write an
anti-comedy is very closely akin to the wish to enclose the stuff
of tragedy within the kernel of comedy.

In the first stage of *Love's Labour's Lost*, Navarre puts forward
an ideal of life which only seems funny because we are in a
comedy: it sounds better in *Il Penseroso*.[24] The members of the
academy which he proposes are to war against 'the huge army
of the world's desires'; they are to make themselves indifferent to
their own affections and to ordinary ambition. Their reward will
be posthumous: the knowledge and wisdom forged in the high,
lonely tower of study will make them 'heirs to all eternity'. It is
thus that they will be victors over death and 'cormorant devour-
ing time'. This dedication to learning is not hollow, or stupid,
or false in itself. But comedy is to encourage a different sort of
victory over death – that spoken of in the earliest of the Sonnets,
say 11 and 12:

> And nothing 'gainst Time's scythe can make defence
> Save breed, to brave him when he takes thee hence.

Berowne is there to mock the solemnity of an ascetic dedication. He is, throughout the play, the spirit of comedy, and of course we are with him as he argues that the academy is against life, against nature, and finally unprofitable: he has no difficulty in demolishing what has scarcely been established. He ridicules severity, and carries the audience with him in justifying the line of least resistance to our desires, and even our sloth. He advances the hedonist case. With an easy contempt, he argues that you do not need to study astronomy in order to enjoy a walk at night. The knowledge men need is not the knowledge that makes a man miserable in its pursuit, but the knowledge which comes spontaneously to those who do not thwart themselves: to those, for example, who are in love:

> Study me how to please the eye indeed
> By fixing it upon a fairer eye,
> Who dazzling so, that eye shall be his heed
> And give him light that it was blinded by.
>
> (*I, i, 80–3*)

To deny women, claims Berowne, is to deny oneself:

> For every man with his affects is born,
> Not by might mastered, but by special grace.   (*I, i, 150–1*)

The last line is excellent doctrine for the holiday afternoon. 'To war against your own affections' (Navarre's words) is useless, but if a vestigial conscience murmurs that passions ought to be mastered, it can be satisfied with the suggestion that the thing will not be done by personal effort, but by intervening heaven: the backslider may enjoy being excused from the contest.

Navarre saw his enterprise as belonging to spring (I, i, 101), but spring should be the emblem of love, not of ascetic study. So Berowne appeals for what is appropriate in life, in terms of seasonal images:

> Why should I joy in an abortive birth?
> At Christmas I no more desire a rose
> Than wish a snow in May's new-fangled shows,
> But like of each thing that in season grows.
>
> (*I, i, 104–7*)

In the end Berowne sociably agrees to take the ascetic vows he knows to be useless.

It is, I think, a mistake to suggest that in this first scene of the play Shakespeare is giving Berowne his personal views on the 'natural' life. It would also be a mistake to see him personally mocking his mocker for his hedonism. There is not really a balancing of opposed moralities here. An enemy of love is put up as a ninepin to be knocked down (beautifully) by Berowne: if we look coldly at the arguments on either side, we might find more to praise in Navarre and less to praise in Berowne than is usually granted. But we are not looking coldly at the arguments: we are in a comedy in which love is paramount and the enemies of love are ridiculous. So far as argument goes, what is specious is true:

> Such is the simplicity of man to hearken after the flesh.

Berowne's arguments are (of course) quickly proved true. The ladies of France arrive and are lodged near enough to the palace to explode Navarre's academy by their very presence. The ascetics fall in love with them. Berowne reflects on his new condition in a famous speech (III, i, 170–202):

> And I, forsooth, in love!
> I, that have been love's whip;
> A very beadle to a humorous sigh . . .

We must take Berowne at his own word that he has been 'love's whip', for we have seen nothing of it. As his role is that of scoffer, we can perhaps accept it easily enough, though the only words he has spoken about love have been in its favour. But why is Berowne so alarmed at admitting what he has argued that all men must admit? Of course, he has taken a vow, and it is humiliating to break it. But the centre of his complaint is not that he has had to admit the force of desire, but that he is in thrall to a romantic infatuation. A corporal in Cupid's army, wearing the colours of his forced impressment 'like a tumbler's hoop', he is serving the 'regent of love-rhymes'. He finds himself romantically in

love and romantically seeking a wife when he has the clarity of
mind to see himself, his desire, and the object of his desire in quite
realistic terms:

> What? I love, I sue, I seek a wife?
>
> A whitely wanton with a velvet brow,
> With two pitch-balls stuck in her face for eyes;
> Ay, and, by heaven, one that will do the deed,
> Though Argus were her eunuch and her guard.
> And I to sigh for her! to watch for her!
> To pray for her!   (*III, i, 186, 193–8*)

Love's Labour's Lost, like *As You Like It*, cannot be understood
at all unless we see, first, the distance between the antics of
infatuation and the straight-forward acknowledgement of the
sexual drive; and, secondly, the inseparability of the antics and
the urge towards sexual satisfaction. Nonsense has been made of
the play by supposing that sweet sentimentalizing and sighing
are *attacked* by Shakespeare because they do not propose the right
true end of love. When Shakespeare writes his sonnets, he may
wish to point out hypocrisy and self-ignorance in the distance
between the protestations of a lover and the *physical* goal of his
longings. But it is another matter in comedy. He is only amused
at the rather extravagant and silly clothes which Desire wears.
A Berowne or a Touchstone will be needed to remind the lovers
in their raptures what their emotion is all about:

> If the cat will after kind,
> So be sure will Rosalind.

It may seem sometimes that as the participants go through the
motions of the mating dance, each one like a peacock spreading
its tail, they forget what all the pretty display is for. But they never
forget for long. Eros leads them into strange capers, but I wonder
if the lovers delude themselves, or fail to acknowledge the physical
side of their love. Cupid's corporals are laughable, but they are
fighting comedy's battle for the peopling of the world.

The sexual 'reality' in the protestations of romantic love is emphasized in the wonderful scene of the unmasking of the vow-breakers in IV, iii. The emblem of romantic infatuation is poetry. When Longaville threatens (to himself) to tear up his poem and 'write in prose' (57), the concealed Berowne mutters:

> Oh, rhymes are guards on wanton Cupid's hose,
> Disfigure not his shop.

There is a case, at least, for the modesty of literary soliciting. But when Berowne has heard Longaville's poem, full of 'goddess' and 'heavenly love' and 'win a paradise', he breaks out in Byronic terms:

> This is the liver vein, which makes flesh a deity,
> A green-goose a goddess. Pure, pure idolatry.
> God amend us, God amend! We are much out o' the way.
>
> (72–4)

There is an unending source of humour, for Shakespeare, in the sentiments and behaviour of young people in love. They may at times be made ridiculous, as they are here. But that is a different matter from attacking them. There are various categories of absurdity as they all go the same way home, and that is about all. 'We that are true lovers run into strange capers; but as all is mortal in nature, so is all nature in love mortal in folly.'

The relations of Armado and Jaquenetta are a comic exaggeration of the comic situation of the comic lovers. Jaquenetta is the Audrey of the play, a very female wench, no more but e'en a woman. Her earthiness makes Armado's affectation all the more ludicrous – 'More fairer than fair, beautiful than beauteous, truer than truth itself, have commiseration on thy heroical vassal.' However ethereal his words, Armado is no more spiritual a wooer than the lords. Unless Costard is shifting the blame, by the end of the play Armado has got Jaquenetta with child (V, ii, 665).

With Berowne's self-awareness as a touchstone, Shakespeare asks us to laugh at the follies of men in love as he intones the mass to celebrate the might and the potency of love. In the end, it is his own priestly office that he attacks.

When the king and his three liegemen are revealed, each one to himself and to the others, as men who (as Berowne promised) cannot abjure or ostracize love, Berowne is asked to find a solace for wounded self-esteem, 'some authority', 'some salve for perjury'. His rationalization (IV, iii, 286–361) is curious (even if we disregard the clear signs of Shakespeare's attempts to revise the speech). He has already given the true justification in IV, iii, 212–16:

> As true we are as flesh and blood can be.
> The sea will ebb and flow, heaven show his face;
> Young blood doth not obey an old decree.
> We cannot cross the cause why we were born;
> Therefore of all hands must we be forsworn.

This is a serious comment. But the long speech of rationalization ('Have at you, then, affection's men-at-arms') evaporates into ridiculous hyperbole. It is a commonplace that Berowne has his special depth in this play from being both the man who participates and also the man who can see the folly of participation. He is that which he mocks. In this speech, the man who can see the affectations of others, and of himself, lunges into a philosophical deification of a green-goose. He really is in 'the liver vein'. Love makes the world go round and inspires fine spirits to fine issues. And the proof of it?

> For when would you, my liege, or you, or you,
> In leaden contemplation have found out
> Such fiery numbers as the prompting eyes
> Of beauty's tutors have enriched you with?

Unfortunately for Berowne's arguments, we have heard these 'fiery numbers' (the lords' efforts at verse) and have joined in the laughter at them. Berowne may be a constant risk to the security of self-deception, but he is also a constant warning that a capacity for self-awareness is no protection against strange fits of folly in a lover. Did Shakespeare revise this famous speech because lines like 'Learning is but an adjunct to ourself' were too good for the hyperbolic rant he intended?

The wooing is now to begin, and the images of war previously used for the battle against the world's desires are now turned in the direction of the ladies of France:

> – Saint Cupid, then! And, soldiers, to the field!
> – Advance your standards, and upon them, lords!
>
> (*IV, iii, 363–4*)

The wooing does not go well: the masque of the Muscovites is a failure, and the lords are baited by their obdurate mistresses. The failure of the masque seems to anticipate the final collapse of the love-quest, but it is not a part of that final collapse. The pattern of 'Love's Labour's Won' can easily include the prostration of humiliated lovers before tyrannical mistresses. The long, brilliant last scene of the play has many anticipations of the reversal which brings it to a close, but none of them really breaks the mood of the conventional love-game. Katherine has a bitter-sweet moment when she remembers the sister who died of love-melancholy; but this is not the real entry of death (14–15). Rosaline promises to 'torture' Berowne, and make him 'wait the season, and observe the times' (60–6); but her relish shows this all part of the love-play and not similar to the final dismissal. Berowne claims to abjure rhetoric ('Taffeta phrases, silken terms precise . . .', 396–415), but the abjuration (half-hearted as it is) is only a stratagem in the siege and is so taken by the ladies; it is later on that Berowne is really reduced to 'honest plain words'.

There is a real faltering in the rhythm of the play, however, when the onlookers wilfully destroy the show of the Nine Worthies, and then the mood of the comedy is once and for all broken by the entry of Marcade with the news of the death of the Princess's father. The entry of 'Death' was wonderfully staged by Peter Brook in his production at Stratford-upon-Avon in 1947. There *was* no perceptible entry: the lights began to grow dim on the laughter at Armado's discomfiture. And as the light on the general scene went low, it slowly grew stronger on the black

D

4 *Shakespeare and the Confines of Art*

figure of Marcade, until he was seen and recognized. The laughter
died away, and he spoke: 'God save you, madam!' For all the
audience could see, he had been standing there for a long time.

Death comes into the play from outside: it is the impression of
every observer and reader of the play. News from a 'real world'
breaks in upon a world of fantasy. The brevity and simplicity of
the exchange of words challenge the whole mood of the play.

> *Marcade:* I am sorry, madam, for the news I bring
>   Is heavy in my tongue. The king your father –
> *Princess:* Dead, for my life!
> *Marcade:* Even so. My tale is told.
> *Berowne:* Worthies, away; the scene begins to cloud.

The princess orders Boyet to prepare for her departure: it is the
play she is leaving, as well as her embassy in Navarre. The king
makes an awkward attempt to keep the play alive: in circuitous
phrases, he pleads that 'the cloud of sorrow' should not hinder the
wooing. 'I understand you not,' replies the princess. And she
really does not understand him, finding no relation between the
world of comedy and the world of grief.

Berowne comes to the rescue; he tries to save the play by
bringing the world of comedy-love into the 'real' world:

> Honest plain words best pierce the ear of grief,
> And by these badges understand the king.   *(743–4)*

We may have been inconstant to our vows and ridiculous in our
actions, he argues. But our folly is a simple consequence of falling
in love. Falsehood to 'our oaths and gravities' has been a discovery
of our true nature:

> And even that falsehood, in itself a sin,
> Thus purifies itself and turns to grace   *(765–6)*

The speech seems to me wholly serious. Berowne, I said, was the
spirit of comedy. We have been playing, he says, even playing the

fool – but this playing is the very heart-beat of our true lives. Comedy moves men through folly towards Thalamos, the culminating YES which starts the world over again.

The princess, preoccupied with the fact of death, insists (as it were) that comedy's celebration of the power of love takes place in a false world. She refuses, without a great deal more evidence, to accept the values and actions of comedy as inhabitants of the world she has moved into. She treats the breaking of the vows (comedy's portrayal of the victory of life over sterility) as real-life offences, perjuries 'full of dear guiltiness'. The king says,

> Now, at the latest minute of the hour,
> Grant us your loves. (777–8)

'The latest minute of the hour' makes us think less of the imminent departure of the princess than of the real clock which shows us that the performance is due to end. The comedy has only a minute in which to right itself into the orthodox happy ending of love granted. But the princess replies,

> A time, methinks, too short
> To make a world-without-end bargain in.

She severs herself from the conventions of the theatre in mistaking the compressed time-scheme of comedy for the clock which actually measures men's lives. The amusing, but very important, confusion between the time-scheme of the theatre and of life is emphasized in the last words of the main characters, when the lovers are dismissed to twelve-months' hard work:

> *Berowne:* Our wooing doth not end like an old play;
> Jack hath not Jill. These ladies' courtesy
> Might well have made our sport a comedy.
> *King:* Come, sir, it wants a twelvemonth and a day,
> And then 'twill end.
> *Berowne:* That's too long for a play.

Literally, a year is too long for a play; literally, a 'minute' is too short a time 'to make a world-without-end bargain in'. But a fictional play is not to have its time-scheme taken literally: the discourtesy of the ladies lies in challenging the value of the symbolic action of comedy. They interrupt the inevitably converging journeys of the play by an appeal to the standards of a harder kind of existence.

It is interesting that the period for which the ladies consign their lovers to the world of suffering is a complete year. Here are the princess's orders to the king:

> Your oath I will not trust, but go with speed
> To some forlorn and naked hermitage,
> Remote from all the pleasures of the world;
> There stay until the twelve celestial signs
> Have brought about the annual reckoning.
> If this austere insociable life
> Change not your offer made in heat of blood,
> If frosts and fasts, hard lodging and thin weeds,
> Nip not the gaudy blossoms of your love,
> But that it bear this trial, and last love,
> Then, at the expiration of the year,
> Come challenge me, challenge me by these deserts;
> And, by this virgin palm now kissing thine,
> I will be thine.   *(784-797)*

A little reading of twentieth-century criticism persuades us that comedy is the advocate of spring's supremacy. In condemning a comedy-lover to a winter of endurance before she will accept his love, the princess almost in so many words asks for proof of the supremacy of spring. Can spring in fact endure winter's attack? When Rosaline forces similar orders on Berowne, neither she nor he expects that the comedy-buffoon can outlast a winter's converse with 'the speechless sick'.

> To move wild laughter in the throat of death?
> It cannot be; it is impossible.   *(845-6)*

The characters and conventions of comedy are being rather brutally treated: they are being asked to withstand the frostiness of our ordinary experience. Canvas scenery is taken outside the theatre and asked to be real mountain and forest. This unfairness is all part of the comedy of *Love's Labour's Lost*: but the humour depends on a scepticism of a kind of comedy whose function is to despise death and belittle its power.

The play ends with music and song, reinforcing the seasonal metaphors for love and suffering, in the form of the age-old debate between Spring and Winter. This dialogue between the owl and the cuckoo, Armado tells us, 'should have followed in the end of our show': Monsieur Marcade forestalled it. One cannot help thinking that the change of mood that has come over the play has affected the music and turned a prothalamion into something very different. Spring comes first with an ironic hymn to fertility: the cuckoo's voice is the voice of adultery.

> The cuckoo then on every tree
> Mocks married men, for thus sings he:
> > Cuckoo,
> Cuckoo, cuckoo: O word of fear,
> Unpleasing to a married ear!

And who has the last word in this comedy? Not spring, even so ironically presented, but winter, 'when icicles hang by the wall'. It is a beautiful song, of course, but winter is still winter:

> When blood is nipp'd, and ways be foul,
> Then nightly sings the staring owl:
> > Tu-who,
> Tu-whit, to-who: a merry note,
> While greasy Joan doth keel the pot.

It is easy to sympathize with those who believe that the reversal at the end of *Love's Labour's Lost* is Shakespeare's way of indicating his moral disapproval of an imperfect and irresponsible attitude to love, delighted with itself and the sweet flurry of words it expresses itself in, but not caring for the real cares of love. For such a view preserves a wholeness in the play as a love-story, and, as Barber says (p. 111), makes it end affirmatively, since the ladies promise to receive the lovers when they have purged themselves of irresponsibility in the real world. But the characters of *Love's*

Labour's Lost are simply not real enough to permit moral judge-
ments about the immaturity of their outlook to apply (I am
reminded of a golden remark about Touchstone: 'his lack of com-
mitment to any way of life makes him incomplete as a man'.)
The contrast in *Love's Labour's Lost* is not between immaturity
and maturity in love, but, as Miss Roesen has made clear, between
the illusion of the world of art, and reality.[24]

By a device of art, Shakespeare tries to subject the world of art
to evaluation in terms external to that world. He behaves unfairly
to the creatures of comedy, not because he thought them lacking
in the sagacity and maturity he might expect of people in life, but
because he wished, in a jest, to protest that a certain form of
comedy was not capable of showing the vicissitudes of things. It
is a formal and not a moral dissatisfaction that Shakespeare shows.
Comedy encourages man with an imitation of life in which love
conquers its restraints, and people move from separation to union
in love. But in *Love's Labour's Lost* Shakespeare challenges comedy
with reminders of death, adultery and pain. A year of suffering
will not go into the 'old play'. He leaves it as a challenge; there
may be weddings at the end of a year. In later works, he
pursues the question: he tries out dramatic forms which can include real pain and yet lead to real union. It is possible that his
next play, after *Love's Labour's Lost*, was *Romeo and Juliet*, in which
he shapes a dramatic form to bring into headlong collision a celebration of the power of love and demonstration of the power of
hate. Before considering that play, I wish to continue this discussion of the comedies.

4

The Abandon'd Cave

The three comedies which show most clearly that development described in the last chapter, from separation through bewilderment to harmony, are *A Midsummer Night's Dream, As You Like It* and *Twelfth Night*. These plays are also distinctive in their note of self-mockery: there is always a voice poking fun at the action. It is not strange that the two characteristics should go together. A successful 'bewilderment' and its resolution ask for a high level of fantasy; it seems a rule with Shakespeare that the greater the fantasy, the more he will call attention to his departures from every-day expectations. Frye remarks of 'a highly artificial comedy' like *As You Like It*, that 'the sense of a show being put on never disappears from the action, and is not intended to do so'.[25] So, as magic or disguise works its confusions, a Theseus or a Jaques, a Feste or a Puck, a Touchstone or a Bully Bottom will be on hand to confirm for the audience their sense of the unreality of what they see.

The most interesting explanations of the presence of so much light-hearted self-questioning in these comedies seem to me those of Frye, in *A Natural Perspective*, and of C. L. Barber, in *Shakespeare's Festive Comedy*. Barber's book, especially in its outstanding chapter on *A Midsummer Night's Dream*, brings forward nearly all the evidence of the spirit of scepticism in the three plays and makes it unnecessary to state the case that this spirit exists. I have said elsewhere that I think the thesis which Barber maintains is too narrow and inflexible: the evidence he brings forward, and the interpretations he makes on that evidence as he goes along, seem to me to need a larger mould than his thesis provides.[26]

Briefly, the thesis is that the action of the 'festive comedies' moves us into the 'release' of the holiday world, with its fantasy, laughter, freedom from care, inversion of diurnal authority. But, by various forms of counterstatement, including the humour of some of the characters which 'places their own extravagance by moving back and forth between holiday and everyday perspectives' (p. 239), a strong idea of alternative values is given, and the comedy moves towards a 'clarification', a deeper awareness of things achieved through the dialectic of the values of release and those of real life.

In his chapter, 'The Triumph of Time', Northrop Frye is not speaking particularly about our three plays. In any well-constructed comedy, he argues, there is a 'minority voice'. Most of the characters participate in the festive mood leading to the crystallization of the new society. But, as in each member of the audience there is that which sympathizes and participates, and that which remains aloof as spectator, so 'there ought to be a character or two who remain isolated from the action, spectators of it, and identifiable with the spectator aspect of ourselves'. These characters, the *idiotes* or clown, suggest also the same involvement in and detachment from the play which is found in the author himself, 'who has both to create and to observe his creation'. The alienated characters exert on the main action a 'force which is either counterdramatic or antidramatic'. 'We get fitful glimpses of a hidden world which they guard or symbolize.'

Frye compares the 'sense of festivity' and the 'sense of alienation' in comedy with pity and terror in tragedy. They need to coexist, for the full catharsis of comedy.

> Part of us is at the wedding feast applauding the loud bassoon; part of us is still out in the street hypnotised by some gray-beard loon and listening to a wild tale of guilt and loneliness and injustice and mysterious revenge. There seems no way of reconciling these two things. Participation and detachment, sympathy and ridicule, sociability and isolation, are inseparable in the complex we call comedy, a complex that is begotten by the paradox of life itself, in which merely to exist

is both to be a part of something else and yet never to be a part of it, and in which all freedom and joy are inseparably a belonging and an escape.

To summarize the continuation of Frye's argument, which is closely woven, and delphic at times, would be a very hard task. He moves forward to the romances, and describes the kind of reality imaged at the end of those plays, 'the world we want'. The *idiotes* figure is changed from clown to villain. If I understand Frye correctly, the challenge of the mocker about the fantasy of comedy's ritual becomes an unacceptable attempt to force the irrelevant values of a non-existent world into the presentation of a new heaven and a new earth.

There is certainly a war going on: a war between that part of the mind which is devoted to the constructs of art and that part which distrusts them. The war is carried on openly and with high humour in the three comedies we are to discuss, but, as Frye indicates, it is not a war confined to a particular type of comedy, or to comedy as against tragedy. And I have tried to show that it is in the sonnets as well. All art is artificial, and any scepticism which Shakespeare may have felt it necessary to include in the 'festive comedies' about the illusion they are built of, or the conduct that is appropriate to them, must also apply to the illusion, and the conventions of conduct, in all his other work. The accumulation of irony in the middle comedies is a difference in degree and not in kind. It is the strength of Frye's arguments that he recognizes the 'minority voice' of the 'alienated spectator' to be more than a special feature of a particular kind of comedy.

A Midsummer Night's Dream begins with separation, when the love of Hermia and Lysander is opposed by great harshness and severity, and the affections of both Helena and Demetrius are unreturned. The young people are moved into the enchantment of a wood in which Oberon and Titania claim (and exercise) very great powers over the harmony or discord of the human world. 'The woods are established as a region of metamorphosis', Barber says, and again, the play 'conveys a sense of people being tossed about by a force which puts them beside themselves to take them beyond themselves' (pp. 133, 129). The magic which, after its own inefficient confusions, miraculously sorts out the unhappy quartet into two loving couples is regarded as a healing work restoring the state of nature. Demetrius forgets his love for Hermia,

> And all the faith, the virtue of my heart,
> The object and the pleasure of mine eye,
> Is only Helena. To her, my lord,
> Was I betroth'd ere I saw Hermia.
> But, like a sickness, did I loathe this food;
> But, as in health, come to my natural taste,
> Now I do wish it, love it, long for it,
> And will for evermore be true to it.   (*IV, i, 173–80*)

The play ends with revelry and solemn blessing for the threefold nuptials – Theseus and Hippolyta, Hermia and Lysander, Helena and Demetrius.

The irony with which Shakespeare views his own creation is brought to a head in the last act, in the famous speech of Theseus, in the mechanicals' play of Pyramus and Thisbe, and in Puck's epilogue. 'The consciousness of the creative or poetic act itself, which pervades the main action, explains the subject-matter of the burlesque accompaniment provided by the clowns' (Barber, p. 148). Shakespeare goes to some trouble to point out the parallel between the 'tedious brief scene of young Pyramus / And his love Thisbe, very tragical mirth', rehearsed and put on by the 'hardhanded men that work in Athens here', for the entertainment of Duke Theseus at his wedding, and *A Midsummer Night's Dream*, put on by William Shakespeare that works in London, probably for the entertainment of a noble couple at *their* wedding.

Theseus wants to be amused, wants to while away the time:

> Come now, what masques, what dances shall we have,
> To wear away this long age of three hours
> Between our after-supper and bed-time?
>
>   Is there no play
> To ease the anguish of a torturing hour?
>
>   (*V, i, 32–4, 36–7*)

From the available entertainments, Theseus rejects a song by a eunuch, rejects the story of a poet being torn to pieces, rejects a satire as 'not sorting with a nuptial ceremony', and chooses a love-drama. The play is to deal with tragic things, but it is promised that it will be amusing enough: the tragedy need not deter those who are looking only for entertainment. The play, as Barber and others have pointed out, has quite remarkable similarities to *Romeo and Juliet*. As it is played, it is a ridiculous travesty of love, death and sorrow as we know them, or think we know them, in real life. And the efforts of the actors are made more ludicrous by their contrivances to make their 'scene' seem real, while at the same time they are reassuring the audience that it is not real (a very curious and subtle mirroring of what Shakespeare is doing in the play as a whole, to create and to undermine illusion at the same time). When Hippolyta expostulates, 'This is the silliest stuff that ever I heard,' Theseus rebukes her gently. All actors (including him and her) are much the same:

> The best in this kind are but shadows; and the worst are no
> worse, if imagination amend them.

Theseus can afford to be tolerant, because he is Baconian; he does not expect more of a play than an amusement to pass the time. The best and the worst play are, like the actors in them, shadows and not substance. What gives credence to the play is imagination; and imagination is suspect in that it 'submits the shows of things to the desires of the mind'. Theseus is not to be deceived into 'believing in' art, and he is not much distressed by the patent foolishness of what Bottom and his friends present.[27]

The evidence for this interpretation of Theseus' position is, of course, in the great speech about the lover, the lunatic and the poet, which immediately precedes the mechanicals' play. Theseus begins by refusing to believe that the things which the lovers report about their adventures actually happened.

> Lovers and madmen have such seething brains,
> Such shaping fantasies, that apprehend
> More than cool reason ever comprehends.

> (*V, i, 4-6*)

We have witnessed the strange adventures and know that Theseus is being unnecessarily sceptical, like Horatio refusing to believe in the ghost. But as soon as, to strengthen his argument, Theseus compares the fantasies of the lovers with the fantasies of a poet, his scepticism assumes an awkward dimension. For, in fact, these adventures of the lovers, which they reported quite honestly, are make-believe: Shakespeare's make-believe. Theseus steps outside the play to question the validity of the poet's vision. He becomes the spectator of the play he is in, as (a moment later) he is the spectator of *Pyramus and Thisbe*, a man not taken in by a shadow-play.

> The poet's eye, in a fine frenzy rolling,
> Doth glance from heaven to earth, from earth to heaven;
> And as imagination bodies forth
> The forms of things unknown, the poet's pen
> Turns them to shapes, and gives to airy nothing
> A local habitation and a name.   (*V, i, 12–17*)

Whether Shakespeare himself thought that 'things unknown' and 'airy nothing' were indeed, as Sidney thought, the highest level of reality, inaccessible to ordinary men, it is the purpose of this book to investigate. But we ought not to let our own admiration for the reality of the poetic imagination colour our interpretation of Theseus' speech. When he says 'nothing', he means 'nothing', and 'the forms of things unknown' are syntactically 'nothing'.

> How easy is a bush supposed a bear!

The centre of Theseus's scepticism is in these lines (18–20) of his speech:

> Such tricks hath strong imagination
> That, if it would but apprehend some joy,
> It comprehends some bringer of that joy.

Mankind, that is to say the poet and his audience, 'would apprehend some joy' – 'apprehend' here in the sense of 'grasp at ' – and mankind uses its imagination to bring that joy to itself, in art. The identification of the shaping fantasies of the lover, the mad-man and the poet in this speech shows Shakespeare preoccupied with the same problems that held him in the Dark Woman sonnets:

> The lover, all as frantic,
> Sees Helen's beauty in a brow of Egypt.
>
> (*V, i, 10–11*)

Love, madness and poetry will all wrest the nature of the thing from what it is to what we would have it to be. The unanswered question is, how do you know what the nature of the thing is? Neither Bacon nor Theseus worries about the possible absence of a standard measure of value or reality. Theseus knows that he can rely on 'cool reason' (line 6). As for Bacon, he seems to have taken Theseus as his master in writing the essay, 'Of Love'. He speaks of 'the mad degree of Love':

> It is a strange thing, to note the excess of this passion; and how it braves the nature, and value of things; by this, that the speaking in a perpetual Hyperbole, is comely in nothing, but in Love.

So of course a state of the emotions which distorts the nature of things is particularly suitable for poetry: 'The Stage is more beholding to Love, than the life of man.'

Puck's epilogue underlines the play's title: think, he says, 'that you have but slumber'd here'. The play has been a dream, a flickering of shadows on the wall. There is no suggestion from Puck, at any rate, that the dream is Adam's, and that we shall wake to find it truth. Earlier in the play he had (as it were) taken up Berowne's words, 'Jack hath not Jill', and turned them round to make what seems a bored comment on the routine of comedy's movement towards wedding and harmony.

> Jack shall have Jill,
> Nought shall go ill;
> The man shall have his mare again and
> all shall be well.
>
> (*III, ii, 461–3*)

I do not think a poet writes *A Midsummer Night's Dream*, or goes on to write so many more comedies, if he shares Theseus's confidence in 'cool reason' or Puck's scorn for the shadow-play which confirms 'country proverbs'. For this reason, I am uneasy with Barber's conclusion that in this play 'mastery comes a little too easily, because the imaginary and the real are too easy to separate' (p. 159), and that 'the confident assumption dominant in *A Midsummer Night's Dream*' is that 'substance and shadow can be kept separate' (p. 161). (His final words seem to allow rather more dignity to what imagination produces, and rather more mystery to the play between one kind of reality and another.) The whole play affirms the power of art, and certain characters and incidents in the play question the power of art.   The balance between belief and ridicule is very finely maintained. Theseus is a shadow questioning the validity of shadows. Shakespeare adopts Kyd's method of 'concentric circles of attention'.[28] The audience gazes down at Oberon and Puck, who gaze down at Theseus, who gazes at the workmen acting out the love of Pyramus and Thisbe. At each level there is confidence and superiority about the level of knowledge that lies below. The method must reflect ironically on the knowingness of the audience about what reality really is. What circle sits above *them*?

The 'contrary valuations' which make both *Love's Labour's Lost* and *A Midsummer Night's Dream* into something like sophisticated debates on the nature of drama are much less evenly balanced in *As You Like It* and *Twelfth Night*. The triumph of love in the former of these, at any rate, is not seriously challenged. The wedding music drowns the 'minority voice' of Jaques, the man who does not wish to press in among the country copulatives. But, though he is laughed at, and excludes himself, Jaques' scorn has some weight.

As You Like It is a perfect progress of all-conquering love. Oppressed people move out into a forest where the Duke can say, 'Here feel we not the penalty of Adam' (if we accept the Folio reading and remember that one of the penalties of Adam was that brother's hand was turned against brother). The forest of

Arden is a limbo in which the personality is freed from the pressure of itself as well as from the pressure of others; the time spent there, yielding to the tide of love among the confusions of concealed identity, is a preparation for the reward of joy. To set foot in the forest is to be charmed into a new and better nature. Dispossession and usurpation are righted at once. Oliver abruptly changes his personality and falls in love. As for the usurping Duke Frederick –

> To the skirts of this wild wood he came,
> Where, meeting with an old religious man,
> After some question with him, was converted
> Both from his enterprise and from the world,
> His crown bequeathing to his banish'd brother . . .
> (*V, iv, 165-9*)

In the last scene, the dispossessed are restored to their inheritance, and lovers are united. There is music, a masque and a dance, with Rosalind as the priestly dispenser of happiness. Since Hymen is 'the god of every *town*' we are moving back, at the end of the play, from limbo into more ordinary habitation, with all the enthusiasm of new spirit.

Jaques is the irrelevant man in all this. In II, v, Amiens brings the charms of music to reinforce the Duke's proclamation that winter in the forest is a spiritual springtime compared with the sufferings of court-life.

> Come hither, come hither, come hither,
> Here shall he see
> No enemy
> But winter and rough weather.

Jaques ridicules the song:

> Ducdame, ducdame, ducdame,
> Here shall he see
> Gross fools as he
> An if he will come to me.

Amiens: What's that 'ducdame'?
Jaques: 'Tis a Greek invocation to call fools into a circle.
        I'll go sleep, if I can; if I cannot, I'll rail against all
        the first-born of Egypt.

I take it that Jaques is deriding songs which help to justify those
who try to escape from society, who imagine that by coming to
the forest they are 'exempt from public haunt'; the songs, as he
sees them, are used as invocations to call fools into a circle. But
the songs in *As You Like It* are also invocations for the audience,
helping to create (very successfully) the spell which takes us into
the world of love fulfilled, where the walls of denial yield to a
gentle push. So perhaps 'Ducdame' relates not to the banished
Duke and his henchmen alone, but to the whole play. Perhaps it is
the title which the cynical Jaques would have given to the play
if he had been in the audience instead of on the stage. '*Ducdame*,
or *As You Like It*; a Greek invocation to call fools into a circle.'
    Jaques is strongly characterized as the non-joiner. The Duke has
fled to a place where the penalty of Adam is not felt, where
brother's hand is not against brother. Like Theseus, Jaques will
not accept the fantasies of the characters, which are the fantasies
of the poet. If the Duke and his followers were in the world of
'public haunt' before, they are so now, though they have changed
their skies. They have not moved out of the world of usurpation
and dispossession: they have simply made a few changes. The Duke
feels some compunction at hunting the deer, the 'native burghers
of this desert city' (II, i, 23); but to Jaques, the hunting is rank
usurpation.

> Indeed, my lord,
> The melancholy Jaques grieves at that;
> And, in that kind, swears you do more usurp
> Than doth your brother that hath banish'd you.
> (*II, i, 25–8*)

They laugh at him for being unable to forget the manners of the
old public world, for so brooding on them that he sees every
happening in Arden as an emblem of the public world or an
extension of the customs of the public world.

> Thus most invectively he pierceth through
> The body of the country, city, court,
> Yea, and of this our life; swearing that we
> Are mere usurpers, tyrants and what's worse,
> To fright the animals, and to kill them up
> In their assign'd and native dwelling place.
>
> (*II, i, 58–63*)

The man who refuses to forget, or refuses to join in a ritual of forgetting, is a comic butt in a play like *As You Like It*, however heroic he might be elsewhere. The Duke does more than laugh at him: he reprimands him for wanting to bring into Arden the unpleasantness of a world which *he* believes he has escaped from. I think that some important points in the conversation between Jaques and the Duke in II, vii, are sometimes overlooked, because attention is focused on the issue of the satirist. Jaques wants to 'speak his mind' and 'cleanse the foul body of the infected world' (60). The Duke is indignant: Jaques would do 'most mischievous foul sin in chiding sin' (64). His reasons are extraordinary: Jaques, he says, has been a gross libertine, 'as sensual as the brutish sting itself,'

> And all th' embossed sores and headed evils
> That thou with license of free foot hast caught
> Wouldst thou disgorge into the general world.
>
> (*II, vii, 67–9*)

It is one thing to say, 'he that is without sin, let him first cast a stone'. It is quite another to say that Jaques would be infecting a pure world by announcing the putrid discoveries he has made in his wild days. The Duke's indignation seems excessive unless we suggest that it is the forest of Arden which he does not wish to contaminate with unpleasant news. A world has been created distinct from the world in which invective and satire have a place. Theseus made a similar rejection:

> That is some satire, keen and critical,
> Not sorting with a nuptial ceremony.

E

Jaques, a gentle Thersites, is not wanted in this play, and he must be mocked. But by inventing and importing him, Shakespeare gives *As You Like It* a positive range and bearing from a play like *Troilus and Cressida*. He calls attention, not to the imperfections of *As You Like It*, because it is surely as near perfection as it is possible to get, but to the exclusiveness, the one-sidedness of the kind of comedy it is. The forest of Arden is to Jaques a false place. It is years before Shakespeare creates its like again: when pastoral reappears in *The Winter's Tale* and *The Tempest*, no Jaques is needed.

Jaques has an encounter with Rosalind in IV, i. He explains to her that his loved melancholy is derived from many sources and from 'the sundry contemplation of my travels; in which my often rumination wraps me in a most humorous sadness'. Rosalind scoffs at him for having seen so much and gained nothing. To which Jaques retorts, 'I have gained my experience.' 'And your experience makes you sad!' replies Rosalind, 'I had rather have a fool to make me merry than experience to make me sad – and to travel for it too.' It makes a nice question: a fool to make one merry, or experience to make one sad? One can make up *sententiae*: 'The price of experience is sadness; to be merry one needs a fool.' Rosalind's choice is decisive, and it is quite right for the play. For us, the 'fool to make us merry' is the play itself, a contrast to our experience. Is 'poetical' a true thing? asks Audrey of Touchstone. 'No, truly,' he replies, 'for the truest poetry is the most feigning' (III, iii, 19–20).

The rest of the scepticism or mockery in *As You Like It* is quite unimportant, considered as a challenge to the power and truth of the art of the play. For all their difference, and the amusement which the behaviour of one may arouse in another, Touchstone, Rosalind, Orlando and Silvius all belong together in comedy's march towards the fulfilment of desire. The love which this play celebrates is wide. *It was a lover and his lass*, that most wonderful of spring-songs, invites the young to sport and tumble in the fields.

> Between the acres of the rye,
>   With a hey and a ho and a hey nonino.

These pretty country folk would lie,
  In the spring time, the only pretty ring time,
When birds do sing, hey ding a ding ding.
Sweet lovers love the spring.

But the songs of Hymen's masque are much more socially cons-
cious: not the license of free love, but wedding and procreation
as the bond of society is their theme.

Wedding is great Juno's crown:
  O blessed bond of board and bed!
'Tis Hymen peoples every town;
  High wedlock then be honoured.
Honour, high honour and renown,
To Hymen, god of every town!

Touchstone's affair comes rather between the two sacraments of
the flush of spring and the solemnity of marriage. He is prepared
for wedlock, since Audrey is unpoetical enough to be honest.
The alternatives are quite clear: 'Come, sweet Audrey, / We
must be married or we must live in bawdry' (III, iii, 99). He
would prefer to have the protection of a contestable wedding
ceremony, but he is ready to accept the conventions of society so
long as he can remain human.

I press in here, sir, amongst the rest of the country copulatives,
to swear and to forswear, according as marriage binds and
blood breaks.   (*V*, *iv*, *57–9*)

Infidelity and adultery are accepted as a necessary part of the
necessary course of human desire. If the play presents an 'idea' of
love, that idea must take in the sighs and rhapsodies of Orlando,
the longings of Rosalind and the realism of 'Ganymede', the
unchastity of the pretty country folks, the 'blood' of Touchstone,
and the hymn to procreation within wedlock. It would be a
mistake to think of Touchstone's bawdy rhymes as a gratuitous
jest at Orlando's expense. They make a necessary anti-masque to
the final wedding music, and give a sexual reality to the sighs of
Orlando and Corin. They bring Rosalind into no smaller a
circle than that of all creatures:

If a hart do lack a hind,
Let him seek out Rosalind;
If the cat will after kind,
So be sure will Rosalind;
Winter garments must be lined,
So must slender Rosalind;
They that reap must sheaf and bind,
Then to cart with Rosalind;
Sweetest nut hath sourest rind,
Such a nut is Rosalind,'
He that sweetest rose will find
Must find love's prick and Rosalind.

(*III, ii, 106–18*)

At the end of the play, when Jaques goes, alone, from the assembly of victorious and united people, to see what the melancholy man of experience can learn from the wicked man who has now chosen a life of devotion, he says,

So to your pleasures,
I am for other than for dancing measures.

He refers to the dance, symbolizing concord, which will now end the play. But the whole play is a dance, in which human conduct achieves a stylized beauty; a ritual which celebrates the victory of love, the healing of divisions. The dance is not broken up as it is at the end of *Love's Labour's Lost*; the ritual is not attacked by the hard head of 'cool reason' as it is at the end of *A Midsummer Night's Dream*; Jaques is content to let the dance proceed, and the partners to keep their hopes. But he has had his say about 'calling fools into a circle', and he has another life than 'dancing measures'.

The exit of Jaques before the dance is, for me, much more poignant than the exits of Malvolio or Shylock. It is in his exit that I feel the force of what Frye says about getting glimpses of a hidden world which alienated characters guard or symbolize. He is going first to the 'abandon'd cave' which the restored Duke no longer needs. The suggestion of revisiting the deserted places in the forest, while the revellers make their way back to the court is a powerful image. They are the places of bewitchment in which comedy granted its gifts to the deserving. At the end of *As You Like It*, Shakespeare abandoned the cave too, for a long period of years. When Jaques reaches it, he will presumably find other visitors there, curious to see the remains of a life they have helped to end, Marcade and Theseus.

For all its vitality and humour, *Twelfth Night* is not only darker than *As You Like It*; it is in many respects an uncomfortable play. Both comedies are plays of liberation. But in *As You Like It* the liberation is by means of escape, whereas in *Twelfth Night* the liberation is by inversion and misrule. *As You Like It* is a parable of healing: from the habitations where there is hatred in families, the characters escape into a magic place which cures malice and provides for lovers their proper partners. In *Twelfth Night*, we remain in the city. Liberation means the temporary lordship of Sir Toby Belch, the subjugation of Malvolio and the deception of almost every character in the play. 'Healing' is an inappropriate word. A brother and sister are re-united by chance, and the initial unhappiness of Olivia and Orsino is resolved in a way that may seem a satire of the 'Jack shall have Jill' theme. Shakespeare, re-peopling an abandoned cave is perhaps a little weary of his duty, and exposes his comedy to questioning at every point.

Morley's settings of the central songs in *As You Like It* and *Twelfth Night* beautifully convey the differences between the plays. *It was a lover and his lass* is the happiest account of love finding its fulfilment in the spring time. What do the lovers themselves sing? Cutting out the refrain, the song goes,

> This carol they began that hour,
> How that love was but a flower,
> And therefore take the present time,
> For love is crowned with the prime.

There is really not much noise of Time's winged chariot hurrying near. Love may be a flower, but it is robustly in bloom at the moment. It is the joy of taking the present time that is dominant, not the fear of growing old. But in the second stanza of *O mistress mine*, the dominance is elsewhere.

Feste sings O *mistress mine* at the height of the saturnalia in
II, iii, the after-hours revelry which is Sir Toby's victory over
care. Sir Toby has of course demanded 'a love song' rather than a
'song of good life'.

> What is love? 'Tis not hereafter;
> Present mirth hath present laughter;
>   What's to come is still unsure.
> In delay there lies no plenty,
> Then come kiss me, sweet and twenty;
>   Youth's a stuff will not endure.

Love is encompassed by darkness here. Love is something seized
to lighten the darkness rather than a free giving and fulfilment.
What's to come is still unsure. In spite of the light ironical tone,
this is jet-black melancholy besides which everyone else's is a
pretty silvered grey. The two songs fall either side of *carpe diem*.
In the first there is no real sense of the menace of time; in the
second, there is no real delight in love. The darkness is visible:
in the first stanza, isn't the lover looking for his mistress in the
dark?

> O mistress mine, where are you roaming?
> O stay and hear, your true love's coming.

As we go on, we hear the voice of Puck ('Jack shall have Jill')

> Journeys end in lovers' meeting
> Every wise man's son doth know.

This is how plays end. When this play is rounded off, with the
meetings of lovers who have (one might say) bumped into each
other in the dark, Feste the clown is left alone on the stage and he
sings his weird plaint as epilogue to the play. The 'folly' which
serves him in a world of play in which Malvolio is the measure
of sanity only antagonizes the world outside:

> But when I came to man's estate
>   With hey, ho, the wind and the rain,
> 'Gainst knaves and thieves men shut their gate,
>   For the rain it raineth every day.

Love is different:

> But when I came, alas! to wive,
>   With hey, ho, the wind and the rain,
> By swaggering could I never thrive,
>   For the rain it raineth every day.

The obscure fourth stanza seems to reflect, like the first three, on the 'reality' of the spheres which were transmuted in the comedy world. Clowning, hostility, love are now followed by drink: 'But when I came unto my beds . . . With tosspots still had drunken heads.'

> A great while ago the world begun,
>   With hey, ho, the wind and the rain,
> But that's all one, our play is done;
>   And we'll strive to please you every day.

Has simplicity and casualness ever been made to convey so much? As Barber says, 'It is the play which is keeping out the wind and the rain.' Or, it is the play which makes the light in the darkness. Not love, but comedy's presentation of love. Experience has made Feste sad, as it made Jaques sad, but he is too urbane, has too strong a sense of humour to go around protesting against self-deception, or to bore the audience with a parade of his knowledge. 'But that's all one': there's not much one can do about the wind and the rain; the world is very old. But there is the play, in which temporarily we shall be liberated from the frown of things or shall live in a world more agreeable to our weakness; and the play will always be there. By art, 'we'll strive to please you every day'.

As Feste's 'minority voice' is more delicate and more subtle, and more far-reaching, than that of Jaques, so the play he is to 'see through' is more vulnerable than *As You Like It*. There is much play, in the Malvolio scenes, about which is the world of sanity and which the world of madness. (The word 'mad' is used more often in *Twelfth Night* than in any other play of Shakespeare's.) The man responsible for decency and order in the household, who has called his opponents mad, is imprisoned as a madman by those opponents. 'You have put me into darkness and given your drunken cousin rule over me.' He protests his sanity to a priest who is a clown in disguise. This comedy world is a very bad dream indeed for the representative of discipline and sobriety. The fantasy of liberation demands that the upholder of authority be simply an object of derision and it is as ridiculous to be sentimental about Malvolio as it is to be priggish about Sir Toby's financial exploitation of Sir Andrew. But it is difficult to respond whole-heartedly to the inversion of the standards of sanity and order, and probably Shakespeare meant it to be difficult. In matters of love, Illyria produces strange miracles. Olivia is quickly jolted out of her role as refuser of love; but she falls in love with a girl disguised as a boy. When Viola's brother comes along she assumes he is her Cesario, and takes him away to church. Sebastian, with as strong a sense of enchantment as his predecessor in Ephesus at this granting of 'love unsought', is content to take his fortune. This mating, if it is seen as the course of true love, is the strangest thing. A woman has fallen in love with a girl, and has somewhat unobservantly married the girl's brother. And the brother is willing to accept a complete stranger as his life-partner. When the truth is revealed to her, she has nothing to say. Sebastian, secure in the bonds of wedlock, is amused, and jests at her mistake (V, i, 266-70), 'explaining' Olivia's error in taking him as nature 'drawing to her bias'. Olivia is, we are told, 'amazed'; but she says nothing; it is very difficult to know what speech Shakespeare could have given her. The sense of restoring nature's bias in the healing of bewilderment works with Demetrius in *A Midsummer Night's Dream*, but Olivia's road to the fulfilment of nature is quizzical indeed.

The lovers' meeting which ends the journeys of Viola and the Duke also has its ironies. 'O mistress mine, where art thou roaming?' Orsino does not achieve his prize, and takes Viola as a second best:

> Your master quits you; and for your service done him,
> So much against the mettle of your sex,
> So far beneath your soft and tender breeding,

And since you call'd me master for so long,
Here is my hand; you shall from this time be
Your master's mistress.   (*V, i, 329–34*)

Viola has certainly won the love she sought, but there is that in the
sentimental and self-regarding Duke which reflects back on her
own quality. D. A. Stauffer wrote of Viola:

> The quintessence of love, in which the personal fever or
> madness has been refined into noble sympathy, is close to that
> charity which Paul exalts in his letter to the Corinthians. In
> Viola, this conception is realized with all the complexity
> possible to developed dramatic art.[29]

But what are we to make of that central scene (II, iv) in which
Viola covertly speaks of her love? 'She sat like Patience on a
monument, / Smiling at grief.'

Orsino, with his voluptuous delight in the 'sweet pangs' of his
own love-melancholy, calls in Feste to sing an 'old and antique
song' that 'dallies with the innocence of love' and 'did relieve my
passion much'. He wants the kind of music which relieves his
passion, not by curing it with surfeit of food, as he extravagantly
demanded in the very first lines of the play, but by feeding it and
sentimentalizing it until his passion becomes a detached object to
commune with and worship.

Feste has no objection to living off the patrons whom he knows
better than they know themselves and he provides for the Duke
the saccharine he will pay for. The melancholy of his song, so
thickly laid on, is poles apart from the real depression underlying
the light irony of *O mistress mine*.

> Come away, come away, death,
>   And in sad cypress let me be laid;
> Fly away, fly away, breath,
>   I am slain by a fair cruel maid.
> My shroud of white, stuck all with yew,
>   O prepare it!
> My part of death no one so true
>   Did share it.

And so on. 'Lay me, O, where Sad true lover never find my grave,

To weep there!' As Feste pockets up his fee and goes out, he gives his blessing to Orsino, 'Now the melancholy god protect thee!' It is in the mood created by Feste, and as an answer to the challenge of her master's vanity about the uniqueness of his own passion, that Viola speaks of her own love through the fable of the sister. Is it not possible that she has learned from a master who is sick of self-love in his own way, and a clown who will minister to the pleasure of heart-ache, to deify or at any rate to give something of a stagey quality to her own emotions?

> She never told her love,
> But let concealment, like a worm i' th' bud,
> Feed on her damask cheek. She pined in thought;
> And with a green and yellow melancholy
> She sat like Patience on a monument,
> Smiling at grief. Was not this love indeed?

The Duke thinks it is. He is eager to complete the story with its proper ending as in Feste's song: 'But died thy sister of her love, my boy?'

I have spoken before of the follies of infatuation, which certainly include the enjoyment of sighs and suffering, as being cheerfully included by Shakespeare in the necessary procession towards Thalamos. 'As all is mortal in nature, so is all nature in love mortal in folly.' But there seems to me a world of difference between amusing absurdity and the kind of mood which Orsino and his pupil are in: a strange sinking mood of abandonment into thinking about passion. The falsity of Feste's song colours the whole 'lovers' meeting' between Orsino and Viola. (I am ignoring the argument that it was not originally intended that Feste should sing this song: we must take the play as we have it.)

What is the truest thing in *Twelfth Night*, if there is a falseness in the lovers and their meetings? Surely it is the greeting of brother and sister, Viola and Sebastian, who had been parted by shipwreck.

> – I had a sister
> Whom the blind waves and surges have devour'd.
> Of charity, what kin are you to me?

> What countryman, what name, what parentage?
> – Of Messaline; Sebastian was my father.
> Such a Sebastian was my brother too.
> So went he suited to his watery tomb;
> If spirits can assume both form and suit,
> You come to fright us.
>   – A spirit I am indeed,
> But am in that dimension grossly clad
> Which from the womb I did participate.
> Were you a woman, as the rest goes even,
> I should my tears let fall upon your cheek,
> And say, 'Thrice welcome, drowned Viola!'
>   (*V, i, 235–48*)

This has been foreshadowed in *Comedy of Errors* and itself fore-shadows the reunions in families broken by shipwreck in *Pericles* and *The Tempest*. It is so much greater, in this play, than the ritual of converging lovers, which seems sardonically treated in com-parison. There was something here to hold on to, when the celebration of achieved love may have wearied Shakespeare.

'According to ancient Chinese lore,' says Huizinga in *Homo Ludens*, 'the purpose of music and dance is to keep the world in its right course, and to force Nature into benevolence towards men.'[30] It seems, on the face of it, a rather useless endeavour. The weakness of studies of Shakespeare's comedy which make too close a relation with its possible primitive predecessor in ritual is that they make Shakespeare too uncritical of the power of sympathetic magic. From a book like Mircea Eliade's *Patterns in Comparative Religion* we learn how orgies and sacred marriages are rituals to assure the regeneration of the powers of nature by one means or another; they show 'the desire to spur on the cir-cuit of bio-cosmic energy, and particularly vegetative energy, on a vast scale'. The rituals, and the myths associated with them, do indeed bring mankind into a living unity with both the natural world and the divine spirit. Eliade has much to say about the orgy in ceremonies of agriculture. He sees them as rituals of 'a temporary return to the primeval chaos, of re-integration into that formless unity which existed before creation'. It is fascinating to see the central bewilderment of Shakespeare's comedies as a version of the orgy, which is the solution of all old sinful forms and the prelude to the manifestation of new ordered form. It is fascinating to think of Shakespeare carving new myths out of ancestral archetypes and to recognize that it is by such myths that men have always given order and meaning to their lives. But if Shakespeare is a modern myth-maker, he has been careful to show us his doubts about his work. The 'festive comedies' do not really end in clarification and in a resolution of the opposing forces of holiday and everyday. A strong magic is created: and it is questioned. I agree with Frye that there can be no incorporation or fusion of the two voices. The minority voice, as I see it, is used to question the deeper value of art, and it is more prominent in these three comedies because, in their nature, they make small attempt to copy what goes on in our ordinary lives, and therefore invite questions about the truth of art.

5

Romeo and Juliet

Twelfth Night is dated by Chambers '1599–1600'. The dating of nearly all of Shakespeare's plays is very uncertain, and difference in mood or tone is often used as evidence of date. But it is not inconsistent with what evidence we have to say that the writing of *Twelfth Night* makes an abrupt end to a certain kind of comedy. Though there are very great differences between *Merchant of Venice*, *Much Ado About Nothing* and *As You Like It*, though there are resemblances between the earliest comedies and the latest Romances, a new world of comedy comes in with *All's Well that Ends Well* and *Measure for Measure*. (*The Merry Wives of Windsor* lies as an incongruity on any chart of Shakespeare's progress.) It seems that the composition of the right comedy was something like a mission to Shakespeare, and that the way forward was through tragedy. But some years before this time, in the middle of the 'nineties when he was writing *Love's Labour's Lost* and *A Midsummer Night's Dream*, Shakespeare had experimented with the fusion of tragedy and comedy in *Romeo and Juliet*. The mixed form of the Henry IV plays, which lets two fictional orderings of the same world play one against the other, is not a fusion. Nor is the very striking effect of including the great figure of Shylock within the comic structure of *The Merchant of Venice* at all similar to the effect of *Romeo and Juliet*.

Romeo and Juliet is a true tragedy, though it is often underestimated. It is a tragedy of a highly original kind, borrowing from *The Spanish Tragedy* the shrinking of the hero's role, and by that means throwing into prominence its web-like structure of many lines of actions crossing each other. But it also belongs with the world of the comedies we have been discussing, as *Richard III* and *Richard II* most certainly do not. It is a celebration of love in a world which continues to be dominated by harshness beyond the limits of the opening scenes. It carries to us the power of love, as the festive comedies do, without making light of all that is against love. We are kept face to face with the energy of love and with the grimness of hatred and death. Though the play does not end with feasting and the promise of procreation, though the lovers themselves are quite defeated of their future, love has shown its quality, and most certainly it wins a victory in society at the end of the play.

The play has that kind of inclusiveness which festive comedy must necessarily lack. A form of drama is found to give equal weight to fertility and sterility; to show that transient love, though soon extinguished, is a permanent thing in the world, and that hatred and violence, though longer lasting by the clock of this world, can be redeemed by the love they destroy.

In suggesting that in *Romeo and Juliet* Shakespeare solves problems which show themselves in the comedies I have written about in previous chapters, I run the risk of seeming to suggest that the more tragic a play is, the more 'real' it is; that *Romeo and Juliet* is better than the comedies because, by emphasizing hatred and death, it frees itself from make-believe. It is rather important to scotch the absurdity at this point. I have ventured the notion (which I believe to be established by the course of Shakespeare's works as a whole) that the good-humoured demonstration of the illusion and make-believe in the festive comedies is a sign of a real dissatisfaction with the relevance of art in men's lives, art considered (that is) as more than an entertainment or anodyne. Now, the illusoriness of art is not going to be conquered by painting the canvas with a darker paint. After all, delight is as real as distress, ecstasy as common as pain. A pessimistic movement in a story (the evidence is vast) may be as facile and as perfunctory as a movement towards a happy ending. *Romeo and Juliet* is in fact a highly contrived and artificial fable. But the illusion which presents in its enchanted glass things which hurt us and make us afraid is mirroring very important parts of our experience, and the illusion which makes light of those areas risks an early disqualification in the contest to provide a form of art which makes sense of our lives. Illusion which limits the range of experience it imitates can hardly appear in the final round of the debate, 'how true is fiction?'. The division of experience into tragedy and comedy, which has more or less disappeared in this century, was bound to be no more than a temporary convenience. Joy on Mondays, woe on Tuesdays. Dr Johnson was not a man to mistake art for life; 'Imitations produce pain or pleasure, not because they are mistaken for realities, but because they bring realities to mind.' Nevertheless, some of his strongest praise of Shakespeare is for his creation of 'the mingled drama', because it approaches nearer than either comedy or tragedy 'to the appearance of life'.

> Shakespeare's plays are not in the rigorous and critical sense either tragedies or comedies, but compositions of a distinct kind; exhibiting the real state of sublunary nature, which partakes of good and evil, joy and sorrow, mingled with endless variety of proportion and innumerable modes of combination.[31]

The 'mingled drama' is something much wider than the fusion of tragedy and comedy which is found in *Romeo and Juliet*, *Measure for Measure*, *The Tempest* and possibly one or two other plays: but Johnson's view holds for the narrower kind. The ways in which drama may be thought 'real' are as vexing to fathom in *Romeo and Juliet* as in *A Midsummer Night's Dream*. But there seems to me no doubt about the fact that *Romeo and Juliet* provides a more inclusive mythos. It could not be a resting place, any more than *Measure for Measure*; the earlier play moves comedy into tragedy; the later moves tragedy into comedy. But each play is a step towards the absolute fusion which was perhaps unattainable.

Romeo and Juliet is clearly a play about two worlds, with the Friar in between, clumsily trying to unite them. The one world is

full of rancour and quite irrational hostility; it accepts the feud
between the Montagues and Capulets as a way of living, and almost
at times enjoys it. Tybalt is the extreme figure in this world.

> What, drawn, and talk of peace! I hate the word
> As I hate hell, all Montagues, and thee!
>
> (*I, i, 76–7*)

Prince Escalus may be able, on two occasions, to stop the fighting,
but his ideal of civil order seems irrelevant to the facts of life in
the two great houses of Verona.

This first world (which we might call the Capulet world) has
an astonishing presumption that, in spite of all the deadly brawling
with rapier, long sword, sword and buckler, the course of social
life will continue smoothly, with suitable marriages for daughters
and natural deaths. These smooth expectations are bizarre in the
midst of the violence which shakes the boards of the stage. Capulet
can break off from discussing the recent outbreak of fighting to
make gestures of sadness about death and of tenderness towards
his daughter in a speech dominated by his delight in his social role
as host at a feast.

> The earth hath swallowed all my hopes but she;
> She is the hopeful lady of my earth.
> But woo her, gentle Paris, get her heart;
> My will to her consent is but a part.
>
> (*I, ii, 14–17*)

Lady Capulet has the same gift for tucking away the obstinate
pressures of our existence within the smooth movement of social
tradition.

> Well, think of marriage now. Younger than you,
> Here in Verona, ladies of esteem,
> Are made already mothers. By my count,
> I was your mother much upon these years
> That you are now a maid. Thus, then, in brief:
> The valiant Paris seeks you for his love.
>
> (*I, iii, 69–74*)

Any pretence of deferring to the child's affection disappears at the first sign of opposition. The Capulet world does not include love, and it is ignorant of the meaning of death. Capulet blows up in anger at the intractable Juliet (III, v, 150-97), but it is in the previous scene, perhaps, that his superficiality is best shown. Against Paris's better feelings, he undertakes to push the marriage forward.

> Look you, she loved her kinsman Tybalt dearly,
> And so did I. Well, we were born to die.
> 'Tis very late; she'll not come down tonight.
> I promise you, but for your company,
> I would have been abed an hour ago. (*III, iv, 3-7*)

In his speech, 'Peace ho! for shame' (which I shall shortly discuss more fully), Friar Lawrence tries to make the Capulets, who understand neither love nor death, realize the hollowness of their world. He halts the wailing and weeping which follow Juliet's 'death'.

> The most you sought was her promotion,
> For 'twas your heaven she should be advanced.
> And weep ye now, seeing she is advanced
> Above the clouds, as high as Heaven itself?
> (*IV, v, 71-4*)

In spite of all the help which she gives Juliet, the Nurse is a part of the Capulet world. She might seem a sort of 'fertility figure', and so a concomitant of Romeo's and Juliet's world of love. With her concentration on sex and death, she might seem to be Mother Nature herself. In her wonderful first long speech, her conversation goes continuously over the themes of maidenhead, marriage bed, pregnancy, suckling, death. But, if the Capulet parents bury love beneath the conventions of socially desirable marriages, the Nurse buries love in an exclusive interest in the woman's role as receiver of the seed and bearer of the child. She is the great good-hearted bawd of the play; it does not matter to her *whom* she brings to Juliet; either Romeo or Paris will do. So we must understand her 'betrayal' of Juliet in that very moving

scene at the end of Act III, when Juliet is left alone. The notion of
sex as a relationship of two persons in love is beyond the Nurse,
and Juliet dismisses her with 'Ancient damnation!', 'Thou and
my bosom henceforth shall be twain.'

The love which forms the second world of *Romeo and Juliet*
needs little description. In Verona we see a great ordinariness,
which is quite blind to the depths of emotion, lodging very
uncertainly on its base of hostility and feud. The love between
Romeo and Juliet seems all the more miraculous for being born
out of this strife and littleness, all the more splendid for holding
itself, secret and complete, an 'entire and perfect chrysolite',
poised above the violent pettiness. Capulet's 'society function',
threatened by the feud, is the setting for a rite of extreme beauty
when Romeo and Juliet take hands, and kiss. The interval to
mark the consummation of their marriage before they appear,
'above', is taken up with Capulet's busy arrangements for
Juliet's marriage to Paris. The play is built on paradox and contrast throughout, all related to two great twin-paradoxes. First,
that two, who are 'enemies' in Verona's eyes should be able to
love, and love so splendidly in so unpromising a world: secondly,
that love should cure hate. Hate breeds love, hate destroys love,
loves destroys hate.

There are several reminders of the love-world of the comedies.
Mercutio's bawdy talk makes him a kind of 'earth' for the rhapsodies of Romeo; he is to Romeo what Touchstone is to Rosalind.
Indecency is a part of the liturgy. These rhapsodies of Romeo do
have their dangers: his exaggerated speeches may make us laugh
at him, or disapprove of him. In the balcony scene (II, ii), his
florid answers are uncomfortable by the side of the direct remarks
of Juliet. These awkward moments ought to be compared with the
exaggerations of love's emotions expressed by so many comedy-
figures, like the men in *Love's Labour's Lost*. The extravagance of
the passionate man can be both mocked and accepted in comedy;
it is less easy to deal with in the more serious play. But a windiness
in words and a rather unrestrained impulsiveness in behaviour in
Romeo serve to put the very youthful Juliet in her proper position
(which reminds us of Rosalind's) in the dance of love. She
serves unwaveringly the truth of her emotions, and is the 'fixt

foot' of the pair of compasses, supporting and controlling the mobile man.

> Thy firmness makes my circle just,
> And makes me end, where I begun.

Juliet, after all, is the truest being in the play, as well as the most important. Everyone is related to her standard, and even Romeo and the Friar suffer in comparison with it.

The idea that the love between Romeo and Juliet might cure the hostility between their two families is prominent in the story from its rendering by Luigi da Porto onwards.[32] It is certainly present in Brooke's poem which was Shakespeare's direct source. In Shakespeare, it is Friar Lawrence's immediate response to Romeo's news:

> In one respect I'll thy assistant be;
> For this alliance may so happy prove
> To turn your households' rancour to pure love.
>
> (*II, iii, 90–2*)

Our thoughts are ours, their ends none of our own. If he were a dramatist writing comedies, Friar Lawrence might introduce his 'orgy' of bewilderment, and show love's triumph at a feast which unites Montagues and Capulets. But he is a character in a play written to show that 'things are not like that'.

The play turns on the scene in which Tybalt challenges Romeo, and both Mercutio and Tybalt are killed. Love and hate come together in a strange chemistry: the explosion shapes the course of the rest of the play. The scene acts as a pivot. A Romeo filled with affection gives soft answers to Tybalt's wrath. But in the Verona world, benevolence is dishonourable cowardice: Mercutio steps in to the fight and is killed when the peacemaker intervenes. Submissiveness cannot survive the death of a friend, and Romeo kills Tybalt. Again, it is paradox on paradox. Love meets hate, and the worst violence of the play comes from the meeting. Romeo is to be banished, and in Friar Lawrence's cell he gives way to his grief. But the Friar is the controller and manager, ready to use his wits to bring good out of evil, and use the force of love to rout the force of hate.

> Go, get thee to thy love, as was decreed,
> Ascend her chamber, hence and comfort her.
> But look thou stay not till the watch be set,
> For then thou canst not pass to Mantua,
> Where thou shalt live till we can find a time
> To blaze your marriage, reconcile your friends,
> Beg pardon of the Prince, and call thee back
> With twenty hundred thousand times more joy
> Than thou went'st forth in lamentation.
>
> (*III, iii, 146–54*)

The Friar's plan is crossed by the decision to marry Juliet quickly to Paris: he conceives the fatal stratagem of the potion, by which Juliet is to appear dead, to be rescued from the tomb when she wakens by Romeo, whom the Friar is to inform and instruct. As we have seen, the Friar uses Juliet's 'death' to try to bring a sense of real values into the lives of the Capulets. He interrupts the extravagant keening with

> Peace, ho, for shame! Confusion's cure lives not
> In these confusions.

His speech is excellent: for the Capulet's attitude to death appears as hollow as their attitude to life. The shame which Friar Lawrence tries to make them feel is very necessary. But there is an awkward feeling that the Friar is playing a dangerous game. He is playing about with death; he too is an ignorant and near-sighted man. It will very soon be shown that *he* does not know where 'confusion's cure' lives; it certainly does not lie within his power. With considerable arrogance, he imposes a fake death on a family, and uses this 'death' to improve and cure them. It is going to take a much greater catastrophe, with real deaths, to bring the family to a sense of reality.

The overturning of the Friar's schemes is often said to be non-tragic: a series of unlucky accidents giving us no sense of inevitability. Friar Lawrence's letter to Romeo miscarries when the messenger is delayed; Romeo hears of Juliet's death and hurries to the tomb. He finds Juliet apparently dead, and takes his own life. Juliet wakes and commits suicide too. Even with the miscarriage of the letter, all might have ended happily if Romeo had arrived a few minutes later, or if Juliet had come round from her drug a few minutes earlier.

To say that there is too much chance here for tragedy is to be doctrinaire. The Friar, in his wider effort to use love to cure hate, has been using death to solve a crisis. The success of his elaborate scheme depends upon the absolute success of each supporting part. The delay of a letter (the commonest occurrence) shows the riskiness of his plans. The catastrophic consequence of Romeo's early arrival again shows what a narrow ridge the Friar was walking on. The Friar's well-intentioned scheme depends on an exclusion of ordinary accidents. When these accidents occur, they throw into a blaze of light the insecurity of human planning. It is not Chance that creates the catastrophe, but over-confidence in one's powers – what the age would have called 'security'. The fact that a happy ending is so very, very nearly achieved ought not to make us grumble at the arbitrariness of an unhappy ending. Its nearness is a quite savage comment on the uncertainty of our deep plots.

The Friar does not see himself merely as 'fortune's fool'. In the tomb, with Paris and Romeo dead, he says:

> A greater power than we can contradict
> Hath thwarted our intents.   (*V, iii, 153–4*)

He does not name the greater power. On the human level, the responsibility is fairly clear. Hate and love brought a crisis which the Friar took it upon himself to solve. However excellent his motives, his contrivances (once they started to operate in the ordinary field of human uncertainty) led directly to the deaths of Romeo and Juliet. All along, with Romeo in the Tybalt affray, and now with the Friar, it is men who have thwarted their own intents. Our intents, and the deeds that belong to them, take very strange shapes as they move from the smooth water of the mind into the wide sea of the world. All action can bring about the opposite of what was intended. Major actions, like the Friar's or Hamlet's, undertaken to cure the world, can bring major disaster.

But, in making so terrible and fatal a confusion by his mis-
guided attempt to mould the course of people's lives, the Friar
does, unwittingly, bring about the end he sought. The families are
reconciled over the bodies of the lovers. The prince sees the loss of
the lovers as God's punishment of the families for their hatred.

> Where be these enemies? Capulet, Montague,
> See what a scourge is laid upon your hate,
> That heaven finds means to kill your joys with love!
>
> (*V, iii, 291–3*)

Capulet and Montague join hands; they speak of the statues they
will raise, and Capulet says:

> Poor sacrifices of our enmity!

It is not at all clear whether the statues or the lovers are the sacrifices: whether he speaks of the monuments as unworthy offerings
which they will make in expiation of their guilt, or of the lovers
as pitiable sacrifices which have been offered up to end the feud.
Whether it is in Capulet's mind or not, the death of the lovers is
a sacrifice: their death was made possible only by love (neither
could bear to live without the other), and it was the only offering
which could bring peace to the families. So the Prologue had told
us:

> – their parents' rage,
> Which, but their children's end, nought could remove.

God is not pushed into the ending of this play as a being who
has caused Romeo and Juliet to be killed in order that their
families should find peace with each other. Nor do the Prince's
words suggest, either, that God has caused the deaths in order to
punish the families. The families have brought the deaths upon
themselves: by a complicated but nevertheless direct chain, they
have caused their children's death. That they should see their
bereavement as their punishment is a religious way of acknow-
ledging their guilt. And no more can be intended by the Prince
or by Shakespeare. Like Kyd, who influences this play so deeply,
Shakespeare leaves the audience to bring what theological interpretation they will to the course of events they have witnessed.

What has passed has its rationale of second causes in the web of human agencies: although nothing depends immediately on the intervention of God, or the stars, the event is so unexpected, awful and mysterious, there is a deep feeling of the presence of 'a greater power than we can contradict.' In the long run, the 'point' is that good has come out of evil: the violent shock of a double death has chastened and pacified, has healed the 'Capulet world'.

The way forward to *Hamlet* is clear indeed, to the play in which the hero realizes the hopelessness of 'deep plots' undertaken to cleanse the world, and comes to believe, that 'there's a divinity that shapes our ends, rough-hew them how we will'. The divinity is not so apparent in *Romeo and Juliet*, but in both plays there is a deep sense of victory emerging from loss and from the consciousness of defeated plans.

Romeo and Juliet surely gives a wonderful sanctity to love. Love justifies itself in its own nobility even without the promise found at the end of comedies. This love exists in – indeed, is born from – a world of malice and pettiness. Malice and pettiness never cease until the shock of death makes the real values of love and mortality apparent. So love has, if not its promise, its triumph. And interweaving with all this is a dramatist's highly artificial patterning of the relation of event to event, utterly different from that which is convenient for the progress of a festive comedy: the patterning of paradox which, showing every intention defeated, powerfully suggests the impossibility of human control of destiny. The final upward turn to the tragic decline suggests (but does no more than suggest) some kind of divine control, or better, of divine rescue. But the divine rescue requires the quality of living and dying that Romeo and Juliet – especially Juliet – have shown.

6

Hamlet

We ought to feel about Shakespeare's royal tragedies what we should feel if we stumbled across colossal statues or megalithic tombs in some remote place. It was a different race of men who created these monuments, and what their purpose was we can hardly tell. These tragedies are far away from our world, and we ought to take it as sufficient benefit that in spite of their strangeness we can still feel them reaching right across into our own lives, that we can still share in the mystery and terror of killing the king. Tragedy, or tragedy of the kind of *Richard II* and *Macbeth*, has gone the way of epic. It seems a mistake to pull these plays about, in books or on the stage, to show how 'contemporary' they are. Their enormous energy and power are only decreased by these efforts.[33] Our own political nightmares need myths which have been created or re-created by our own writers: why turn cathedrals into government buildings?

The pattern of royal tragedy varies greatly, but killing the king seems to be at the centre. In *Richard II*, the king, inviolable and semi-divine, is degraded and rejected; locked in a prison and done to death. The play is about pollution, and it is about purification. It is built on a chiasmus: as royalty is degraded, the royal man rises as man. In *Richard III* we have the royal impostor, who must be hunted out and destroyed, if the kingdom is to survive. In *Julius Caesar*, we are not sure if we have the desecration of the king and the hounding of his killers, or the doing away with the impostor followed by society's vengeance on its best man. *Macbeth* gives us double measure, with the sacrilege of regicide so intensely conveyed in the murder of Duncan, followed by the killing of the impostor.

Hamlet is a royal tragedy, and ought to be seen as one of these megalithic plays of antiquity, in spite of its astonishing power to haunt every generation, in spite of its certainly being 'modern' as Arnold described it, showing 'the dialogue of the mind with itself', the self-torment of the intellectual.[34] It is a play about killing the king, a play about the ordeal of the long quest to strike down the royal impostor.

Ivor Brown has made the alarming suggestion that the genesis of *Hamlet* might have been at a meeting of the sharers of the Chamberlain's Men in 1599:

> The pressing question is Will's next move. More history? Falstaff again? Or another king? Shakespeare is flattered, but disconsolate at the prospect of further delving into the chronicles of Hall and Holinshed. Can't he have a change? Somebody, perhaps Burbage, says that the Hamlet story has always been popular: revenge plays usually please: why not a new version of Hamlet by the best writer of the day? The notion is acceptable. Shakespeare has had it vaguely in mind and agrees to turn it over in a practical way.[35]

But would it matter even if it were so? The quality of what Shakespeare creates seems hardly to be affected by the material pressures which may have made him start out on a given play. Whatever pushed him into writing *A Midsummer Night's Dream* or *As You Like It* or *Hamlet*, his creativity was free enough to make these plays landmarks in the progress of the unfettered artist.

Whether or not *Hamlet* rose (and rose is the word) from the deliberations of Mr Brown's committee, Shakespeare certainly found his freedom in service of another kind, service to the inner idea of the revenge play as Kyd had created it in *The Spanish Tragedy* (and conceivably also in the earlier version of *Hamlet*). The only essential reading for *Hamlet* is (besides *Hamlet*) *The Spanish Tragedy*. This latter play is, like *Hamlet*, always moving to and fro between 'play' and 'reality'. All the action is watched by an audience on stage, who come from the other world. Near the end of the play, the actors themselves become an audience for Hieronimo's play, a play in which the miming suddenly becomes 'real'. In Peter Weiss's 'Marat/Sade' play, actors play the parts of lunatics, and a play about the French Revolution is put on, which the inmates watch and join in: the revolutionaries are thus made to seem lunatics, and the real audience see themselves as both potential lunatics and potential revolutionaries. In Kyd's play, actors become an audience, and the real audience see themselves as actors, or puppets watched over by cynical observers from the underworld.

In *Hamlet*, too, the 'play' at the end (the fencing-match) becomes, like Hieronimo's play, the greatest reality in a drama in which all previous serious action seems, in its ineffectiveness, to be mere play. Moreover, Hamlet's playlet in Act III, is (as Harry Levin has argued) 'a working model of the play itself':[36] it is the means by which Hamlet objectifies the uncertainties surrounding his life, and brings home to Claudius, one of the audience, a new sense of the meaning of what he has done. The whole play is Shakespeare's objectification of uncertainties, and an appeal to the theatre-audience to accept it as reality. The vital difference between the handling by Kyd and Shakespeare of the 'play/life' confusion is that in Kyd the accent is on life as a mere play, and that in Shakespeare the accent is on playing as being, in some way, life itself.

The core of *The Spanish Tragedy* is Hieronimo's sense of relation with the divine will. Hieronimo sets out to right a wrong, and make justice operate against the doers of evil who have killed his son. He is a lonely figure to begin with, and he becomes more and more isolated, except for the help of Bel-Imperia, as the play goes on. The conventional justice of society is shown to be a hit-or-miss affair, and Hieronimo fails to bring it to his assistance. For a moment, he is not sure whether he ought not to leave things to heaven, but he goes forward to exact the final penalty from the murderers himself, feeling certain that heaven, which must hate the murder of Horatio as he hates it, and must wish for the punishment of Lorenzo and Balthazar, supports him in his lonely endeavours. But, as mere man in a world which Kyd has shown to be filled with the ironic inversions of human plans, he brings

about a different end from the triumphant cleansing, explanation
and self-immolation which he intended. Bel-Imperia kills herself,
his attempt to hang himself is thwarted, and the play ends with a
sordid scurry of violence, in which a crazy revenger bites out his
tongue and murders the innocent Castile before stabbing himself.
The watchers from the shades smile as they see the conclusion of
a train of events in which Hieronimo and his great quest were
only an interlocking part.

It is never certain how far Hieronimo was right to feel himself
approved of by heaven as he went forward. In the much earlier
revenge play, *Horestes*, by John Pickering (1567), it is the Vice,
the diabolic joker, who tells the hero that his desire to take
vengeance on his guilty mother is sanctified by heaven's approval,
yet Horestes is an honest and sympathetic character. Hieronimo
is not clearly aided either by God or by Satan. For his part, he has
the strong consciousness of divine providence. The audience is
left in sheer uncertainty; it strongly sympathizes with Hieronimo
and his course of action; there is a victory for justice as the murderers are destroyed; there is a strong sense of the impossible complexity of human affairs, as an attempt to cleanse the world ends
so clumsily. We feel that a man has done his best in a world where
it is impossible to do well, and that, if his faith that he was fulfilling the divine will goes beyond the evidence, there is no
evidence either that he was going against the divine will; nor is
there evidence that there is a divine will to fulfil or to defy.[37]

Hamlet is a play, not about *inaction*, but about *action*; about the
timing of action, and what it is that action will bring about.
Hamlet continuously talks about these two things, and other characters join in. Claudius says,

> That we would do
> We should do when we would, (*IV, vii, 119–20*)

and Polonius 'replies',

> Give thy thoughts no tongue,
> Nor any unproportioned thought his act.
> (*I, iii, 59–60*)

of his mission, and tries to convert his mother from her shame. But even this visitation of the Ghost, to remind him that his duty has been defined elsewhere, fails really to show Hamlet the folly of his sense of freedom.

When he is, a second time, given his opportunity, and time and events have purged him of his conviction of personal power, he takes it, but it is at the cost of his own life. And he himself has caused his own death, since Polonius's death leads to the madness and suicide of Ophelia, to Laertes' revenge, and hence to the fatal fencing-bout.

> Rashly,
> And praised be rashness for it, let us know,
> Our indiscretion sometime serves us well
> When our deep plots do pall. And that should learn us
> There's a divinity that shapes our ends,
> Rough-hew them how we will.   (*V, ii, 6–11*)

Nothing is more certain, to Hamlet and to us, than that his 'deep plots' have palled. It is unnecessary to quote his sayings in this scene with Horatio which give us the strong sense of his belief in providence lying in every incident and accident. 'Why, even in that was Heaven ordinant,' he says of the chance that he had with him his father's signet which enabled him to restore the official seal on the commission of Rosencrantz and Guildenstern which he had broken open and changed. 'The readiness is all.' Readiness to accept what comes, readiness to act rashly and impulsively, in the understanding that every occasion has its purpose, every action its place in a grand design. At the end, the suddenness of the occasion for killing the king, and the suddenness with which he takes it, bear out the beliefs he has come to.

What is the difference between obeying a rash impulse, thereby killing Polonius by mistake, and obeying a rash impulse in order to fulfil the will of heaven? Nothing at all – except in the condition of the person. The native hue of resolution has little enough to commend it, in itself. But to the man who has seen through the folly both of thoughtless action, and of action too carefully, too proudly and too confidently planned, there is the way between. The man who has examined his conscience and has faith that his general course is the course that God wills, the man who comes to find in humility his sense of identification with Heaven, may know that it will not be through his contrivances and plans that God will work, but through the ordinary accidents of life and the ordinary sudden impulses of man. So, at any rate, I understand Hamlet's belief in the last act of the play.

What is implied, I think, is not the sense of all the actions of humanity being the planned progress of divine intention, but the tense of God's using the anarchic tussle of deeds and fallings-out so bring about what He desires:

> There's a divinity that shapes our ends,
> Rough-hew them how we will.

The concept is surely much like that which emerges from the disasters of *Romeo and Juliet*.

There is no doubt that the world's scene, as *Hamlet* presents it, is an 'unweeded garden'. There is neither direction nor meaning, and man is helpless enough:

> So shall you hear
> Of carnal, bloody, and unnatural acts,
> Of accidental judgements, casual slaughters,
> Of deaths put on by cunning and forced cause,
> And in this upshot, purposes mistook
> Fall'n on the inventors' heads. All this can I
> Truly deliver.
>
> (*V, ii, 391–7*)

But, among all this, the upright man has received a visitation from another world and been given his task. He makes a sorry enough confusion out of his task. But, in the end, when two ships pitching and rolling in the strong seas close their gunwales for a moment – like Hamlet's ship and the pirates' – the upright man can board in the instant. The readiness is all. There is the possibility then of the cleansing act which pays for all, the killing of the impostor-king.

It is a solitary gesture and a momentary triumph, but it is an action seen in its 'true nature'. After such an achievement, which, as we have seen, could in Hamlet's particular case only be made after an entanglement which costs Hamlet his life, death is a deep peace. Hamlet was not ready for the victorious action until such time as his death was inevitable; but by that time, death is a longed-for release. Once again, there is a purification which is only to be brought about by sacrifice.

How much did Shakespeare himself believe of the interpretation of life which *Hamlet* seems to present? It is quite impossible to say, not because the play in the least lacks the air that it was 'meant', but because *Troilus and Cressida* and *Othello* cut the lifeline which *Hamlet* proffers – and *Othello* in its turn demolishes the cynicism of *Troilus and Cressida*. What *Hamlet* does surely show, what *Troilus and Cressida* and *Othello* and *Romeo and Juliet* with their quite different 'answers' also show, is the kind of world which art has to try to reduce into order and meaning. Whatever Shakespeare *believed* about ultimates, he impresses on us most definitely what he *knew* about contingencies and accidents and the failure of intentions, about the breaking of promises, about malice, treachery, lust and death, about hostility and cruelty, despair, misunderstandings and hypocrisy. He knew about other things, too, about friendship and conscience and love and the sense of justice, and pity. What does he do, but write plays in which his deep sense of these things is apparent, and in which the shape of the play dictates to these things their own place in a significant universe? To write these plays is to believe in the transformations of experience which these plays work. 'Do you suppose for one moment that Shakespeare educated Hamlet and King Lear by telling them what he thought and believed? As I see it, Hamlet and Lear educated Shakespeare.' So Yeats wrote to O'Casey.[39] In the comedies we have examined, disbelief enters even into the writing of the play. And disbelief enters even a tragedy like *Hamlet*. It enters through the image of play which is so striking. The play is the truest thing we have – but it is only a play. The play is a manner of believing, but it cannot permanently satisfy; if it did there would be no more plays.

Shakespeare may have taken up *Hamlet* because Burbage

suggested he should: it doesn't really matter. If he accepted the
suggestion, it was because the revenge-convention as Kyd had
established or consolidated it gave him a vehicle for exploration.
He seized upon that vital centre of the long quest for vengeance
during which the avenger becomes convinced that heaven supports his endeavours. This life-line for the solitary avenger becomes a life-line for the audience. A tantalizingly difficult life-line,
certainly. If we can grasp it, we have got, to set against drift and
confusion and the avenger's human errors and crimes even, the
sudden possibility of the intersection of a firm transcendent world
with the infirm human world in an act of terrible justice, only
available at the cost of the avenger's life. Both *The Spanish
Tragedy* and *Hamlet* explore the limits of what the individual missionary can achieve in a world of anarchy. Both plays concentrate
intense sympathy upon the missionary, in spite of all the wrong
turnings he takes. Each play, with its own different emphasis,
hints strongly at the intertwining of divine will and individual
mission. Shakespeare leaves much less uncertainty than Kyd does
about the relation between heaven and the avenger. But some
uncertainty is there. It is surely right that the presence of the
divine, and the very nature of the divine, should be left clouded.
Otherwise the full tragic value of the play with its sense of
mystery and sense of hope, might evaporate into cheerful confidence. Shakespeare gives us the possibility of divine rescue, not
its certainty.

Our sense of doubt ought not to extend towards the killing of
Claudius: the doubt is about the presence in the world of divine
meaning and the possibility of linking with it. Whether we feel
that God is present or absent in the world of the play, the death of
the impostor-king is necessary (if he is legally the king he is
morally the usurper). Some modern criticism has failed to identify
the object it observes, in making Hamlet something approaching
an unreclaimed, un-Christian savage, egged on by a Ghost who
probably came from hell.[40] I am sorry to make so large a disjunction between art and life, but our feelings about the operation
of the *lex talionis* and capital punishment in our own society have
very little to do with the mythic material of a sixteenth-century
revenge-play. It is much, much better to yield ourselves to the

material, than to accept the only alternative, which is, not to protest against Hamlet as immature and un-Christian, but to demythologize, or dematerialize the final killing, and say it is a symbolic act of social purification.

7

The Problem Plays (i)

The order usually given for the composition of Shakespeare's plays in the first five years of the seventeenth century is *Hamlet*, *Merry Wives of Windsor*, *Troilus and Cressida*, *All's Well that Ends Well*, *Measure for Measure*, *Othello*. It would not matter very much if this order were decisively unsettled. Because between the writing of *Twelfth Night* and *King Lear* we have what is best seen not as a steady development but as a single period of intense experimentation. Any attempt to see among these plays the enlargement or modification of some 'view of life', the progress of cynicism or faith, hope or despair, is bound to fail. One play contradicts another. Hamlet and Bertram, Cressida and Desdemona are not figures on different rungs of the same ladder. They stand apart, each looking in a different direction. The old-fashioned view of Shakespeare's being at this time in some great trial of spirit is not to be laughed out of court. But the old-fashioned language will not do: Shakespeare was viewed in Carlylean terms, moving from the Everlasting No to the Everlasting Yea; he became the typical Victorian sage, losing his faith and recovering equipoise through Wordsworth and the simple pieties of life. Perhaps Shakespeare was always standing on the brink; but in the years we are talking about, the danger of falling into the gulf seems much greater. The task is what it always has been: to organize the disorganized, to give meaning to the absurd. But the problem plays (to use that awkward but unavoidable term) give us the sense of the enormously greater difficulty of the artistic organization at this middle-stage of Shakespeare's career. It seems no longer possible to set up a superb comic fantasy and laugh at its one-sidedness, or in tragedy to give to destruction its sense of solemnity and its consolation. One drastically new form after another is taken up and discarded. A play now can be a resounding dramatic failure, filled to the seams with magnificent material which cannot be accommodated within the chosen shape. He requires a fiction which will digest all he knows, and there is tumult in his attempts, in these few plays, to create it.

> For no thought is contented. The better sort,
> As thoughts of things divine, are intermixed
> With scruples, and do set the word itself
> Against the word.   (*Richard II, V, v, 11–14*)

In writing *Troilus and Cressida*, Shakespeare *may* have been influenced by some special, private audience, more sophisticated and better educated than the public audience at the Globe; he *may* have been influenced by the satirical tone of other plays belonging to this time. Audiences and analogues are as important in studying Shakespeare as Irish history is in studying Yeats; one might even say they are the vessels which hold the liquid and give it its shape. But they can't help to describe the flavour of the liquid, and when they are hypothetical (as they are not with *Hamlet*), it may be a mistake to spend too much time on them. For the flavour of the liquid, one might turn to a discussion like that of the late Una Ellis-Fermor in *Frontiers of Drama*, though some may find the wording rather intense. The essay on *Troilus and Cressida* made a very deep impression on me in 1945 when the book was published and it will be clear how thoroughly Miss Ellis-Fermor's reading of the play has influenced my discussion, particularly in matters of the relation of form and meaning, of the 'idea of disjunction' between 'conduct, ideals and event' being 'a fundamental principle' of the play, and of the thought of the play as 'an implacable assertion of chaos as the ultimate fact of being'. Differences in interpretation are frequent enough, but I gratefully acknowledge a major debt.

If *Hamlet* is a thing of antiquity, *Troilus and Cressida* strikes us as astonishingly contemporary. Its basic valuation of life, and the improgressive design which embodies the valuation, seem very familiar in the mid-twentieth century. There is no hero; the mood of the play varies between uneasy comedy, prolonged debate, and disaster which cannot rise to tragedy; the plot jerks from the love-theme to the war-theme, from the Trojans to the Greeks. Almost every important person in the play tries to find a star to follow to give meaning to the circumstances he is in, and every star proves a will-o'-th'-wisp. Like the two tragedies previously discussed, the play insists on a lack of relation between intention and event, but in this play there is no sense of divine rescue from human muddle. In a way the play is anti-art, because its very structure is a kind of defiance of the continuity, consequence and unity which the more usual kind of play will provide. Shakespeare dispenses with the suggestion of order and meaning which a unified plot with a single hero must impose on any material. His reasons for doing so are in the matter of the play.

In the first scene of the play, there is an amusing moment when Troilus, irritated by the unromantic earthiness of Pandarus's attitude, and irritated that he has no means of moving forward towards Cressida except by the efforts of this man, tries to lift himself up by his fancy into a rosier world.

> O gods, how do you plague me!
> I cannot come to Cressid but by Pandar,
> And he's as tetchy to be wooed to woo
> As she is stubborn-chaste against all suit.
> Tell me, Apollo, for thy Daphne's love,
> What Cressid is, what Pandar, and what we.
> Her bed is India, there she lies, a pearl.
> Between our Ilium and where she resides,
> Let it be called the wild and wandering flood,
> Ourself the merchant, and this sailing Pandar
> Our doubtful hope, our convoy and our bark.
>
> (*I, i, 97–107*)

Troilus is in just the same situation as the Greek leaders are shown to be in the third scene, at a stay in their affairs and trying by the exercise of words to invest themselves and their circumstances with a dignity which it is made quite clear they do not possess.

In this famous third scene, the sense of immobility and paralysis is strong: the war will not go forward, and Achilles stubbornly stays in his tent. The elaborate language of Nestor's and Agamemnon's speeches raises the Greeks from an exasperated army stuck in the mud to a band of heroes proudly abiding the tests of heaven –

> the protractive trials of great Jove
> To find persistive constancy in men.

Ulysses enters into this fantasy of self-congratulation with all the skill of the politician, sprinkling flattery widely before he begins his long speech on 'degree'. Commentators are only just beginning to see this speech which, when extracted, is an admirable poetic statement of Elizabethan ideas as a speech spoken by a dramatic character at a particular moment for his own special purposes.[41] Ulysses will not float off into complacency, like Nestor and Agamemnon. He knows that 'Troy in our weakness stands, not in her strength.' And he knows the cause of weakness: it is disobedience, and contempt for leadership. Ulysses is the man who believes that craft and cunning will *work*. He believes that 'policy' – intelligent stratagems – can rule human affairs (the progress of his device for bringing Achilles into action is one of the main subjects of the play). He really is very angry with Achilles for despising the politic mind, which alone engineers the future.

> They tax our policy and call it cowardice,
> Count wisdom as no member of the war,
> Forestall prescience, and esteem no act
> But that of hand ...
> .. The ram that batters down the wall,
> For the great swing and rudeness of his poise,
> They place before his hand that made the engine,
> Or those that with the fineness of their souls
> By reason guide his execution.
>
> (*I, iii, 197–200; 206–10*)

Ulysses has several purposes in his magnificent speech on 'degree'. First, he wishes to insist on the necessity of obedience, since only by obedience can the framer of policies carry his plans into action. Secondly, as a support to his first purpose, he wishes to attach to the Greek leadership a divine authority: for though he may, perhaps, consider his own role in leadership more important than that of others, his own usefulness depends on a general sense of awe towards the high command, especially Agamemnon. Thirdly, he wishes to do, in a much more effective way, what Nestor and Agamemnon have done in their speeches. The latter seemed to assure their companions that nothing was wrong: this is a short-sighted way of encouraging morale. Ulysses can encourage morale while pointing to their own faultiness and frightening his hearers with a vivid picture of the consequences of anarchy: he encourages morale by drawing a picture which shows the Greeks as *potentially* a glorious society in harmony with the universal law.

The great set-piece on 'degree' is followed by Ulysses' description of Patroclus's scurrilous mimicry of Agamemnon and Nestor. It is this description, as much as anything, that gives us the impression that in the degree-speech Ulysses is working for a particular effect. Much depends on the producer here: the caricatures of Nestor and Agamemnon as Ulysses describes them ought to have an embarrassing resemblance to the men as we have seen them behave on the stage. Pandarus as we see him has little to do with Troilus's ecstatic picture of him. Nestor and Agamemnon as we see them have little to do with

> the glorious planet Sol
> In noble eminence enthroned and sphered
> Amidst the other.

If there is a feeling that Achilles and Patroclus are awkwardly near the truth in their derisive view of Nestor and Agamemnon, should we not also wonder whether they have some share of the truth in their mockery of Ulysses himself and his 'policy'? It is worth pursuing Ulysses' role to the end of the play, because the demonstration of the collapse of his values is much less commented on than the collapse of the ideals of Troilus and the romantic Trojans.

Ulysses' 'policy' is demonstrated in his careful scheme to use the chivalric challenge of Hector to shame Achilles into action. Ajax is to represent the Greeks; Ajax is to be built up and Achilles' pride is to be tumbled. As the plan progresses, Ulysses arranges for the Greek leaders to pass by Achilles' tent and treat him slightly or indifferently (III, iii). Achilles wonders at the change of attitude, and Ulysses comes in to strike while the iron is hot. The whole scene is a particularly interesting turning-over of the question, wherein lies a person's value?, which is so prominent in the play (very obviously, as regards Helen). But the essential point is that the whole of Ulysses' moralizing and philosophizing, including his second magnificent set-speech ('Time hath, my lord, a wallet at his back'), is based on a situation that he himself has engineered. There is a great deal of talk about the wayward nature of life, illustrated by the rise of Ajax and the decline of Achilles, a great deal of moralizing. It may be good moralizing; it may represent Ulysses' beliefs, but the fact remains that Ulysses, as in the degree-speech, is not here to speak truths but to pull Achilles into action. He has contrived a situation, he pretends that this situation is a touch of nature, and he uses it to persuade Achilles.

The ruse works: Ulysses' 'policy' is successful – up to a certain point. Achilles says,

> I see my reputation is at stake,
> My fame is shrewdly gored.   (*III, iii, 227–8*)

His 'mind is troubled, like a fountain stirred'. When he meets Hector after the inconsequential duel with Ajax, he speaks insolently of the way he will kill him in the field on the next day. So Ulysses has won: 'Tomorrow do I meet thee, fell as death,' says Achilles. But Thersites brings him a letter from Hecuba with a token from Polyxena, his 'fair love', engaging him to keep his word not to fight. Service to his love asserts itself as a greater duty than service to his country:

> Fall Greeks, fail fame, honour or go or stay;
> My major vow lies here, this I'll obey.   (*V, i, 48–9*)

So Ulysses has failed. When the fighting starts, Achilles is not in the field, but sulking in his tent. And not only has Ulysses failed

with Achilles but his elaborate scheme has so built up Ajax'
pride that *he* is refusing to fight! Thersites sums it up

> The policy of those crafty swearing rascals, that stale old
> mouse-eaten dry cheese Nestor, and that same dog-fox
> Ulysses, is not proved worth a blackberry. They set me up in
> policy that mongrel cur Ajax against that dog of as bad a kind,
> Achilles. And now is the cur Ajax prouder than the cur
> Achilles, and will not arm today, whereupon the Grecians
> begin to proclaim barbarism, and policy grows into an ill
> opinion.   (V, iv, 9–18)

The Grecians begin to proclaim barbarism: that is to say, they
announce that the best 'policy' is untutored nature, not the deep
plots which go awry. And they are quite right. What brings
Achilles out into the field at last, savage enough to wreak the
final blow on the Trojans, is anger, anger for personal loss, in
the death of his 'male varlet' Patroclus. Ajax too comes into the
field in a burst of emotion, at the loss of a friend. So Achilles at
once illustrates the indecisiveness, inconstancy and impulsiveness of the people in this play (Troilus, Hector, Cressida) and the
vanity of deep schemes to pull human affairs into a required
shape. W. B. Stanford, pointing out that Ulysses' failure was
part of the tradition, suggests that it shows that reason is powerless
here because it meets passion and pride, and protests that the
failure could not 'have been intended to vilify him'.[42] Ulysses is
certainly not vilified, but nowhere in the play is reason shown to
have effect. It is irrelevant in the development of events, and the
purpose of the Ulysses-theme in this play is to show what had
been shown in *Romeo and Juliet* and *Hamlet*, that reasoned plots
are useless.

The play is rather remorseless in its showing the collapse of
hopes, ideals, beliefs. It seems to circle about the Object, exchang-
ing one valuation for another, and demonstrating their invalidity.
It is remarkable how the face of things changes, as we move from
one character to another. Pandarus has a wonderful commonness
of valuation: to see Queen Hecuba through his words, shaking
like a jelly with laughter and wiping the tears from her eyes!
It's like *Bartholomew Fair*. Agamemnon with his complacency,

Aeneas with his courtly chivalry, Troilus with his romantic enthusiasm, Ulysses with his realism, Hector with his earnest sense of absolute value, Thersites with his cynicism – they are all looking at the same world, and not one of them, by means of his perception or belief, can satisfactorily explain it or control it.

The sense of meaningless drift is strongly present in the very fact of the great Trojan council scene. The Greeks have been shown in paralysis: but their question is how to complete the action they have undertaken. For the Trojans, however, after all these years of war, the question is, are we right to be engaged in this war at all? The need to find their actions explainable, related to some outer standard, is almost pathetic. Hector argues that their actions are wrong; the motive for the war is Helen, and Helen, weighed in the scale of absolute value, is an insufficient motive: therefore the war should cease.

> 'Tis mad idolatry
> To make the service greater than the god.

Troilus argues that valuation is personal: they have valued Helen as worth a war, 'she is a theme of honour and renown'. Even if their opinion has changed, honour is a sufficient reason to justify their continuing the war: that is to say, it would be dishonourable to disown what they have once owned, and dishonourable to turn about and conclude an ignominious peace. So Hector makes his famous volte-face.

> If Helen then be wife to Sparta's king,
> As it is known she is, these moral laws
> Of nature and of nations speak aloud
> To have her back returned. Thus to persist
> In doing wrong extenuates not wrong,
> But makes it much more heavy. Hector's opinion
> Is this in way of truth. Yet ne'ertheless,
> My spritely brethren, I propend to you
> In resolution to keep Helen still,
> For 'tis a cause that hath no mean dependence
> Upon our joint and several dignities.

The play constantly tells us of inconstancy. In the very first scene, Troilus comes in resolved to fight no more, and goes off at the end of the scene to join the battle, seemingly unaware that he has changed his mind. Cressida vows fidelity –

> The strong base and building of my love
> Is as the very centre of the earth,
> Drawing all things to it –   (*IV, ii, 109–11*)

but to seal her infidelity she actually woos Diomed. Even among all this, the gulf between belief and action in Hector is startling, and one never comes to it without a shock, however familiar one may be with the play. He has his opinion 'in way of truth', backed up by the sacredness of what the 'moral laws of nature and of nations speak aloud'; yet he embraces a course of action that is quite opposed to his opinion.

In Hector's mind, something like the debate between More and Hythlodaye in the first book of *Utopia* must be going on. The question there is whether the good man with his better knowledge should join in the council of kings, to try to improve the 'corrupted currents of this world'. Hythlodaye argues the uselessness of joining in: 'a man can have no occasion to do good, chancing into the company of them which will sooner pervert a good man, than be made good themselves'; society must be changed before men can be changed. More, however, argues that it is necessary to compromise in this world: 'You must not leave and forsake the commonwealth'; the aim of the wise man is, 'that which you cannot turn to good, so to order it that it be not very bad'.[43] Opinions will differ on the morality of Hector's conduct, but it seems to me that he has freely chosen the course which More (ironically?) makes himself advise in that great debate. One's knowledge 'in way of truth' may be, quite simply, useless in the world of men and the actions they are engaged in. It is not in cowardice, but with a kind of heroism that Hector gives up the impossible task of remonstrance and persuasion, and goes forward with his fellow-men. In a very different situation, Troilus said of love that 'the will is infinite and the execution confined, that the desire is boundless and the act a slave to limit'. Truth is truth for Hector, but the act is a slave to limit. But if he thought, in the decision for war made out of fellowship, 'so to order it that it be not very bad', he thought vainly. He fights with courtesy and chivalry – witness his sense of brotherhood in not continuing the duel with Ajax (IV, v, 119–35), his mercifulness as Troilus describes it (V, iii, 39–42), his courtesy to Achilles (V, vi, 13–15). But he is killed by an offence against the law of arms as he himself practices it: Achilles and his Myrmidons set upon him when he is unarmed, many against one, and slaughter him. It is a cruel death in more ways than one. Hector continued fighting in a war he did not believe in, but he was not aware of the real conditions of the war he chose. His rash pursuit of the coward (in V, vi) because his 'sumptuous armour' had taken his eye was possibly included by Shakespeare as a comment on his fatal lack of understanding of the true nature of war. But, when all is said, he failed because he had too much confidence in the goodness of men. Ajax said to him, 'Thou art too gentle and too free a man.'

We need spend very little time on the irrelevance of Troilus's beliefs to his position because the whole matter is so very obvious. We see him constantly 'braving the nature of things' with hyperbole, living in the intoxication of a fantasy about love and the object of his love which is pretty far removed from the nature of the relationship, and from the nature of Cressida. When eventually he is forced to see her as Ulysses immediately sees her, as a 'daughter of the game', his disillusion shares something of the romantic hyperbole which has characterized his illusion. In a renowned and brilliant speech, he refuses to believe that his Cressida and Diomed's Cressida can be the same person (V, ii, 137–60).

> If there be rule in unity itself,
> This is not she . . .

> The bonds of heaven are slipped, dissolved and loosed.

A person who has argued against absolute standards of value and has made a case that all worth is relative and subjective is now claiming that the inconstancy of Cressida has shattered his belief in standards based on supernatural authority. All that Troilus ought to infer from what he sees is that he personally has been mistaken in his estimate of the woman he loves.

The end is bleak. A disillusioned and grim Troilus announces the death of Hector. 'Hector is dead, there is no more to say.' There is cold comfort for the doomed city in

> With comfort go.
> Hope of revenge shall hide our inward woe.

Pandarus comes in to jest with 'traders in the flesh' about his venereal diseases, and with his rhymes the play closes.

What is the 'true' valuation of things which the play suggests, against which Ulysses' practicality, Hector's sense of absolute value and his courtesy, Troilus's belief in the holy power of love, are shown to be irrelevant and inoperative? The malcontent Thersites, with his reduction of human conduct to 'Still wars and lechery! Nothing else holds fashion. A burning devil take them!' is extreme in his bitterness, as one would expect of the disappointed idealist which essentially he is. The contempt of Diomedes for both Greeks and Trojans, and his sense of the waste of human life in fighting for a whore, is again a personal valuation.

> For every false drop in her bawdy veins
> A Grecian's life hath sunk; for every scruple
> Of her contaminated carrion weight
> A Trojan hath been slain.   (*IV, i, 69-72*)

But in these two men, who (however cynical their conduct may be) expect something better of humanity than they find, there is something much nearer the picture of what actually happens in the play, than in the words of any other character. Both the war-theme and the love-theme in the play rest upon a core of sensuality and female infidelity. The lightness of two desired women, Helen and Cressida, is the basis of the entire action. In the war-theme, we have two groups of men, in the middle of a long war, transfixed by different kinds of paralysis. The Trojans, debating even now whether the war is worth fighting, can achieve nothing decisive with their chivalric code of war with honour. The Greeks, crippled by disaffection and insubordination, can achieve nothing

even with the resources of rhetoric and contrivance which lie in
Ulysses. It is the sudden anger of Achilles, and his cruelty, which
bring about the only forward movement of the play; that, and the
lubricity of Cressida.

The picture, since it is the author's selective picture, is its own
evaluation. The question is, whether this picture of human affairs
moving forward only by infidelity, impulse and cruelty is
presented as a decline from what might be, or as a statement of
what has to be. That Shakespeare might wish things were better
is one thing: but that *Troilus and Cressida* is a warning against sin,
or an encouragement to better planning of social life, is quite
another. What does it show of the better paths men might follow?
'I speak no more than truth', says Pandarus; 'Thou dost not
speak so much!' retorts Troilus (in the first scene) – and we all
have the same retort to the play. Anything is better than a
cynical Shakespeare. But, for the moment, it is what the play
says, not what Shakespeare says. I have tried to show that the
substance of the play shows the incongruity and irrelevance of
every attempt to make acceptable sense of the happenings, and
of every attempt to gather together and control the happenings.
There is a distance shown between men's beliefs, plans, vows, and
what actually happens, which the play maintains is not bridge-
able. Anyone is free to disagree with the unpromising conclusion,
but disagreement ought not to affect interpretation of a play
which says that men cannot do what they choose, or even be what
they choose. The sense of human inefficacy is common enough
in literature, and is common in Shakespeare as we have already
seen. What distinguishes *Troilus and Cressida* from pretty well
every other play of Shakespeare's that deals seriously with men's
helplessness is the absolute lack of any sense of non-human guid-
ance. If the 'degree-speech' had come at the end of the play, its
appeal to a divine harmony of society which men wilfully disrupt
might give us a tragic idea of at least the possibility of co-operating
in a better order of life. But, like the sonnet, 'Poor soul, the
centre of my sinful earth', it does not come at the end, and what
is made to follow shows it to be sadly inappropriate: you just
cannot lift up the facts of humanity in *Troilus and Cressida* from
the level of Hobbes to the level of Hooker.

8

The Problem Plays (ii)

All's Well that Ends Well and *Measure for Measure* are twin plays, and at the heart of each there is a real discomfort, which is, finally, a question of form. There seems no doubt that the two plays, presenting comedy's old mating dance with an immense difference, are Shakespeare's attempt to recreate comedy. The fables are as bizarre and 'unlikely' as ever they were, with their incidents from folk-tale, like the healing of the king and the substitution of the bride, and the complicated contrivances which give to the happy endings an air of prestidigitation. These wonder-working matters are, however, accompanied by a deep plunge into very serious moral problems. Modern criticism has established beyond disproof that there is in these plays, intertwining with the far-fetched plots of comedy, a Christian or near-Christian pattern of providence and redemption. Shakespeare himself steps into our twentieth century arguments that the rhythm of his earlier comedies is essentially a religious rhythm and shows quite clearly that the movement from disaffection and difficulty through formlessness to a state of harmony can certainly be an emblem of achieving grace.

The first requirement in the new kind of play is to give comedy real wounds to heal; or rather, so to present the wounds that comedy must heal that they seem real to us as the wounds of loss and suffering in the earlier comedies did not seem real. Generalizations are awkward, and many will feel that the wounds in *Much Ado about Nothing* and *The Merchant of Venice* are presented in a way that affects us more deeply than anything that happens to Helena or Bertram in *All's Well*. Nevertheless, the gravity of tone in dealing with crisis and difficulties in *Measure for Measure* is quite new in Shakespearian comedy, and I feel much more kinship in tone between *Measure for Measure* and *All's Well* than between *Measure for Measure* and any earlier play. The second requirement in the renewed comedy is to transmute the concluding harmony: where formerly wrong-doers like Oliver reformed and took their place in society, there is now a sense of sinners being saved; and it is certainly not too much to say that as the joy of human marriage and procreation is quietened at the close of these plays, there is the hint in the wooing of Bertram by Helena, and of Isabella by the Duke, of the betrothal of heaven and earth. The difficulties, bewilderment and concord of the festive comedies are all immeasurably deepened: comedy expands to include more of the grimness of this world and more of the mystery of the next.

Yet these two plays are failures. Each fails in its own particular way, and each has a greatness which perhaps compensates for the failure, yet failure there is in the two of them which is very different from the failure of *Troilus and Cressida*. The latter play purposely fails to answer the expectations of the audience for a pattern which will explain and console. The failure of *All's Well* and *Measure for Measure* is in their insistence on a happy ending in spite of the evidence.

Shakespeare's many changes from his source in composing *All's Well* include the bringing in of the Countess of Rossillion, Lafew, and Parolles, and the expansion of the King's part. Thus he heavily builds up the older, 'guardian' generation, and places Bertram as a man pulled by two cords: one attached to his dead father, the other to a Vice, Parolles. The conflict between youth and age in this play has been dwelt on by E. M. W. Tillyard and G. K. Hunter.[44] People are always speaking of the need for Bertram to live up to the standards of his father and his father's generation, and to maintain by his conduct the family honour (it is made clear at the beginning that Helena lives up to *her* father's example). 'Youth, thou bear'st thy father's face . . . Thy father's moral parts Mayst thou inherit too!' says the King. Unlicked

youth going out into the world with the example of his pre-
decessors pushed at him so much may well feel the insistence on
his responsibilities very tiresome. Bertram is constantly supported
by Parolles ('that same knave That leads him to these places') in
giving in to himself, or taking the easy way out.

The idea that lies behind the narrative is of youth as formless
potentiality, with a vessel to give it noble form in the example of
the past, but also with a tempter to pull it astray into sinful
forms. But if there is a tempter there is also a protector, to save
youth from itself. The protector is there to reclaim what has gone
astray, and the method by which the protector works is not to
forestall or to cancel out, but to turn evil intentions into good
results. This method of protection, which does not stop men being
bad if they will, but prevents the consequences by altering the
situation, is also at the heart of *Measure for Measure*. It is the justification of the bed-trick, and the reason for its use. Bertram and
Angelo fall and try to do wrong; a protector intervenes, so that
their fulfilment of their wrongdoing is, in the event, a fulfilment
of good. The method is a highly artificial and emblematic way of
presenting the gulf between intention and result and the sense of
rescue from human muddle, discussed in earlier chapters. In its
meaning, however, this stylized rescue is the stuff of normal
Christian thinking. Surrounded by exhortations, strong enough
to stand but free to fall, falling, but – O *felix culpa* – able to be
saved from the consequences of sin by the intervention of heavenly
grace: such is Christian man and such is Bertram.

There is not much chance of missing Helena's role as heavenly
agent. She heals the King, and the whole incident is accompanied
by references to Heaven:

> He that of greatest works is finisher
> Oft does them by the weakest minister . . .
>
> Of Heaven, not me, make an experiment . . .
>
> The greatest Grace lending grace . . .
> Health shall live free, and sickness freely die.
>
> Heaven hath through me restored the King to health.
> (*II, i, 135-6, 153, 159, 167; II, iii, 64*)

The Countess says, when Bertram has deserted his wife and she
has set off in contrite pilgrimage:

> What angel shall
> Bless this unworthy husband? He cannot thrive
> Unless her prayers, whom Heaven delights to hear
> And loves to grant, reprieve him from the wrath
> Of greatest justice.   (*III, iv, 25–9*)

The symbolism of the ring shows clearly what is at stake and
what is achieved. The getting of the ring is part of the ordeal
Helena has to succeed in; 'When thou canst get the ring upon my
finger which never shall come off . . .' The ring is a family heir-
loom (III, vii, 22–5) and therefore represents that traditional
honour which is itself a symbol of a state of grace. Bertram knows
its value:

> It is an honour 'longing to our house,
> Bequeathed down from many ancestors,
> Which were the greatest obloquy i' th' world
> In me to lose.   (*IV, ii, 42–5*)

But he gives the ring away to the girl he is trying to seduce.
Helena, however, is at the back of it all, fulfilling the ordeal,
taking into her own safe-keeping the honour Bertram is prepared
to give away, getting and guarding the ring until she can wed
him again with it.

All this is straightforward enough. But is Bertram saved?
Suppose we take the vital scene in which the tempter, Parolles, is
unmasked and discredited (IV, iii). It is a prose scene, and the
words of the anonymous lords are big with the theological
burden of dismissing the Vice and redeeming Bertram. 'There is
something in 't [the Countess's letter] that stings his nature, for
on the reading it he changed almost into another man . . . Now
God delay our rebellion! As we are ourselves, what things we are.
Merely our own traitors . . . [Helena] made a groan of her last
breath, and now she sings in Heaven . . . The web of our life is
of a mingled yarn, good and ill together . . .' The not-very-
pleasant picture of the callow Bertram which the play has built

up is quite transmuted by the long generalizing conversation between the two lords; he becomes in the talk of others what he has never appeared to the audience, a human creature, weak and errant, but God's creature, and apt for redemption. But the entry of Bertram destroys it all; it seems like a joke at the lords' expense, a laughable commentary on their vision of frail man fit to be saved. He comes straight from his assignation with 'Diana'.

> I have tonight dispatched sixteen businesses, a month's length apiece. By an abstract of success, I have congied with the Duke, done my adieu with his nearest, buried a wife, mourned for her, writ to my lady mother I am returning, entertained my convoy, and between these main parcels of dispatch effected many nicer needs. The last was the greatest, but that I have not ended yet.

This jaunty indifference to the relative values of things takes one's breath away. E. M. W. Tillyard surely let his fancy run away with him when he wrote, 'It has been a heavy series of blows, but for the moment he keeps control of himself and bluffs it all out with a brutal callousness and a bravado which we know conceal an inner qualm.'[45] We know nothing of the kind. As he watches the unmasking of Parolles, we hear nothing from him to suggest the man in whom the necessary shame and contrition can possibly lodge.

The behaviour of Bertram in the final scene of the play is not a matter for critical debate: debate arises in placing it in an interpretation of the play. His behaviour is agreed to be execrable. While he thinks he is safe, and has put not only Helena but Diana out of his mind and is looking forward to marrying Lafew's daughter, he can cheerfully ask pardon for his 'high-repented blames' (36). As he is driven into a corner, he lies and lies again, slanders Diana, until, with the entry of Helena, there is no way out. Upon the revelation that his wife is alive, that he has lain with her and got her with child, he asks pardon, handsomely enough perhaps, but very briefly – 'Oh, pardon!' – and promises to 'love her dearly, ever, ever dearly'. It is all done in two-and-a-half lines on his part. In his New Arden edition, G. K. Hunter says, 'If personal reconciliation is really the end of this scene, we can only say that Shakespeare has been extraordinarily clumsy.' He argues that Shakespeare is less concerned with personal reconciliation than with ransom and forgiveness, but that nevertheless Shakespeare has quite failed to find the note here to give life to the spirit of mercy and new life, as he was able to in the Romances (p. liv). The argument is persuasive, but there is perhaps a hint in Professor Hunter's admirable study that we prefer the play that Shakespeare meant to write but somehow didn't. He remarks elsewhere (p. xxxvii): 'The point of reconciliation is only reached by self-sacrifice, by an acceptance of oneself as outcast and despised; this acceptance of death, leading to fuller life, is something that Helena, the Countess, the King, Parolles, Diana all have to face in turn; *that the pattern is not fully achieved for Bertram is the major thematic failure of the play*' (my italics). It is surely true that there is a major failure in *All's Well* connected with the treatment of Bertram in the end, but is it right to speak of it quite in this way?

The treatment of Parolles shows us a scoundrel changed by shame into a new recognition of himself and a new way of life. Bertram is not so treated. Helena never saves Bertram. He is unredeemable: Shakespeare could not save him. It is not a matter of failing to write the lines that would have changed the soul of the play: it is a matter of not being able to force one's conscience to alter a character whose alteration would be, simply, incredible. Angelo's alteration in *Measure for Measure* is an entirely different matter: he has all the resources for change, the depth of being, that the shallow Bertram never has. In *All's Well*, the unconvincing words, asking pardon and promising love, are all that can be wrested from the figure Shakespeare has created. Anything further would be falseness and he surely knew it. He has driven the play to a fold it cannot enter, and he refuses to make it enter. That is the failure. But why the obstinacy of the character of Bertram? Has Shakespeare 'accidentally' created the wrong figure for his story? The obstinacy is in humanity as Shakespeare saw it before it is in his dramatic fiction. Given a providence, given a whole world of family honour to guide him, given the angel-like wife to safeguard him from the consequence of his actions, the imbued irresponsibility, selfishness and shallowness of a Bertram remain intact.

I do not suggest that the intractability of Bertram in the last scene is Shakespeare's irony: a satirical comment, that is to say, on the idea of redemption which, we have seen, the play unmistakably presents. Theologically speaking, it may perhaps seem so. But I can see Shakespeare, filled with the idea of salvation and bold enough to put it into terms of comedy, finding at the end that there are portions of humanity which could not come within *his* vision of the scope of salvation. And there always will be, in Shakespeare's plays, that slag or clinker which the purging fire will not consume – most notably imaged in Caliban.

Shakespeare's honesty has then, in a way, wrecked the play: the final harmony is in fact discordant. The need he felt to tune that discord is seen in the composition of *Measure for Measure*. Yet to have wrecked the play as a comedy is still to have produced a work which speaks out even more truth than the completed circle could have shown. There is a consolation somewhere in the failure to bring off the consolation for the audience. Shakespeare has met the challenge he gave to his own earlier comedies, and wrought a form of comedy which would be more inclusive of the facts of evil. He refuses, at the last minute as it were, to believe that he can contain the facts within the form: if the play disappoints, we are surely deeply impressed by the sense of struggle and by the honesty of the craftsman who tries to bring the deep hopes of the soul into the images of art, and finds them countered by the even deeper doubts.

There is no need to speak at length about a play that has been so fully discussed in recent years as *Measure for Measure*. It contains some of the greatest things that Shakespeare ever did. Yet it creaks horribly. I have argued that it succeeds where *All's Well* 'fails'. The penitence of Angelo and the reception of the new man into the society of the play is convincing and moving.

> O my dread lord,
> I should be guiltier than my guiltiness
> To think I can be undiscernible

> When I perceive your Grace, like power divine,
> Hath looked upon my passes. Then, good Prince,
> No longer session hold upon my shame,
> But let my trial be mine own confession.
> Immediate sentence then, and sequent death,
> Is all the grace I beg.   (*V, i, 364-72*)

Shakespeare mutes the triumph of the ending. Though he
achieves the cure of Angelo, he does not stretch credibility with
the equivalent of fishing Antonio's wrecked ships out of the ooze
at the end of *The Merchant of Venice*. The Duke went away in
order to see if a stricter regime could change the infamy of Vien-
nese life. The strictness becomes morally impossible when the
strict judge discovers and sets free his own sensuality. Mercy and
forgiveness, it is demonstrated, are a nobler way than severity
and the letter of the law. But, at the end of the play, the Duke's
problem is still on his hands. Speaking in the person of the Friar,
he says at:

> My business in this state
> Made me a looker-on here in Vienna,
> Where I have seen corruption boil and bubble
> Till it o'errun the stew.

Except for the alteration of Angelo and the taming of Lucio
(and there was not much corruption in him), things go on as
before. Mary Lamb ended her heroic attempt to re-tell *Measure
for Measure* for children in this way:

> When she became Duchess of Vienna, the excellent example
> of the virtuous Isabella worked such a complete reformation
> among the young ladies of that city, that from that time none
> ever fell into the transgression of Juliet, the repentant wife of
> the reformed Claudio.

It is just this wiping clean of the slate which Shakespeare avoids.
Another part of his restraint in the happy ending is contradicted
by Mary Lamb. Shakespeare does not tell us that Isabella is
going to become Duchess of Vienna. The Duke clearly proposes
marriage twice in the last scene (490, 532-4). But Isabella does not

reply. The suggestion of betrothal is as far as Shakespeare wished to go, and it is a much richer thing to leave it there, half earthly and half unearthly, than to take it further and make this novice nun agree at the first beckon from the Duke to surrender that virginity she has so insisted on preserving.

The ending of the play then seems very successful in achieving a new kind of harmony for comedy. The first half of the play is also, unquestionably, brilliant. As a drama of choice and decision, with the two main characters discovering their own souls as they act upon each other, there is nothing like it in all the rest of Shakespeare's work. Both Angelo and Isabella are trapped by their own kind of idealism: each attempts to do away with human compromise and to live by absolutes – the absolutes of law or of chastity. Each, in reaction to the other, makes his great decision: the austere judge to violate Isabella, the austere nun to refuse her maidenhead as a price for saving her brother's life. In all this the individual has full responsibility for what he does. No witches, no Iago, no ghost, no Cassius. Both Isabella and Angelo are quite alone: Isabella at least has the fire and ice of her faith and convictions to guide her; Angelo, poor man, is not even alone with himself; the 'self' has crumbled at the approach of Isabella and he has nothing at all to direct and control the tide of his lust.

But at this point in the play (III, i, 151), when Isabella's self is about to crumble as well under the stress of meeting her brother's pleas for his life, we are thoroughly cheated. We are never shown the consequences of the two great decisions. Responsibility for choice and for the consequences of choice are taken out of the protagonists' hands as the Duke steps in and labours to find an alternative female body for Isabella's and an alternative severed head for Claudio's. The *theory* of the thing is well enough: and criticism has dealt only too fully with it. In the terms I have used earlier in the chapter, it is a question of a character charged with heavenly power moving in to protect men from themselves, converting evil intentions into good results, and shielding the weak and the oppressed.

But in practice we have been given the kind of drama which will not be interrupted by stage-images of heavenly intervention. What we really want to know is, what happens to a person who decides as Isabella decides. Does she relent? Does she harden? If she relents, what do she and Angelo feel after their union? If she hardens, what happens to her? She was already hysterical when the Duke intervened.[46]

There is no question of Shakespeare's being constricted by his story. He deliberately altered his sources to bring in Mariana and the bed-trick. He chose to alter the whole spirit of the dramatic movement from lonely human choice to the devices and intrigues of a controlling superhuman figure. The awkward moments are all well known – Isabella's readiness to assent to the bed-trick, the 'Friar's' confidingness about the confessional, the decision not to hang Barnadine and the convenient death of Ragozine, the difficulty of maintaining the dignity of the Duke against Lucio's gibes. All these passages are uneasy and awkward for the same two reasons: first, the incompatibility of the intrigues of comedy with the tone of what has gone before, and secondly, the incompatibility of these intrigues with the providential protection they are meant to be emblems of. An example will make this last point clearer. For the full effect of the last scene, so that Isabella may show the strength of her forgiveness by pleading for a man she believes to be a murderer, Shakespeare needs to keep her from the knowledge that her brother has been saved. So he makes the Duke give a good reason for not enlightening her.

> She's come to know
> If yet her brother's pardon be come hither.
> But I will keep her ignorant of her good,
> To make her heavenly comforts of despair
> When it is least expected. –

> Isabella: Hath yet the Deputy sent my brother's pardon?
> Duke: He hath released him, Isabel, from the world.
>   His head is off, and sent to Angelo.
>   (*IV, iii, 106–10; 113–14*)

In the first place, this is a downright lie. But we almost forgive it in comparison with the appalling justification of the lie. 'To make her heavenly comforts of despair!' God works in mysterious ways, but this beats all – willingly to cause despair in order to show the beauty of divine consolation. The distance between the contrivances necessary for the fulfilment of the comedy and the workings of God which they are meant to suggest is impossibly great.

The Tempest shows just where Shakespeare fails in *Measure for Measure*. It is not that he has included subjects too grave to be solved in terms of a comic or tragicomic structure, or that the idea of a *dramatis persona* controlling events with more than human power is too much for a play which meets good and evil head on. *The Tempest* has such a unity of spirit that we never feel cheated when events are suddenly arrested and changed by external power. And Prospero can maintain all his roles as exiled Duke, magician, father, controlling providence without one making another look ridiculous. *The Tempest* has unity, but *Measure for Measure* is a hybrid. The great idea of deepening comedy, of trying to make the comic form contain the facts of tragedy, is not achieved by the graft of comedy on to tragedy half-way through a play. The comedy-fabric, as Shakespeare has woven it in *All's Well* and *Measure for Measure*, is simply not strong enough to bear the weight of the human problems pressed on to it, nor the weight of their religious solution. He seems not to be able to convince himself, and he does not convince us, that the Christian idea can fully come alive within the tragicomic form. The plays can only be kept heartwhole by methodical criticism which treats them as allegories, which they certainly are not. The problem of moving grave crises towards a fortunate conclusion without giving a feeling of awkwardness is still not near to a solution.

9

The Jacobean Tragedies

To try to explain even what problems Shakespeare set before himself in each of his great Jacobean tragedies, let alone comment on what he achieved, would be to try to write the Definitive Book, which is as illusory as El Dorado or the Holy Grail and as painful to pursue. The great differences between *Othello, Lear, Macbeth, Antony and Cleopatra, Coriolanus* and *Timon of Athens* are in themselves sufficient evidence that Shakespeare was all the time in motion, exploring, conquering, failing, moving on. Of the six tragedies, *Macbeth, Antony* and *Coriolanus* do not, however, give us the same sense of Shakespeare's dissolving all things to bring them together in some quite new way as *Othello, Lear* and *Timon* do, and rather than peck at all the plays, I shall speak at length only about the last three. Though the argument can well be followed through the others.

Antony and Cleopatra is a positive demonstration of the 'contrary valuations'; it is the play Shaw recognized, 'a faithful picture of the soldier broken down by debauchery, and the typical wanton in whose arms such men perish',[47] and it is also the more generally recognized tragedy of supersession, of the ousting of the old richness and generosity by the colourless efficiency of youth, a 'faithful picture' indeed of a decline which makes the hero's partner, blessed even in her riggishness, rise to a nobler quality of being. The play is equally these two pictures: not one first and then the other. It is an Egyptian obelisk testifying to the impossibility of single vision and simple judgement. At the same time, it makes little attempt to explain the world. Like its companion Roman plays, it is not in the least theological: the diabolic infection so dominant in *Othello* and *Macbeth* is quite absent, and so is the continuous suggestion of heaven which we find in *Macbeth* and *King Lear*.

Macbeth, on the other hand, may be thought too placidly theological. It is no worse a play for accepting a traditional and conventional explanation of evil, but in comparison with other plays it seems fundamentally to accept more than to question. Certainly it is no worse a play: it is even possible that its almost unflawed greatness is achieved because Shakespeare took the Faustian structure and, freeing himself from the strain of freedom, was able to devote himself to creating the greatest of all Faust-like plays. A hero of rich imagination and high ambition is worked on by emissaries of the devil; to achieve his ambition he commits a crime which is against God and nature; he reaps only spiritual despair from his material gains; he suffers retribution at the hands of the emissaries of God and departs to damnation. This is the skeleton, and on it Shakespeare puts the flesh and blood of *Macbeth*. In this play, the man who questions whether life has any meaning is a man who has trusted the devil; the man who sees all life as so much strutting on a stage is a man who has sinned against the light. Macbeth in his existentialist nightmare ('Returning were as tedious as go o'er') and Macbeth in the transcendent vision of the meaninglessness of the process of time ('Tomorrow and to-morrow and tomorrow . . .') provide moments of intensity not easily paralleled. We usually tell students that the despair crystallized in

It is a tale
Told by an idiot, full of sound and fury,
Signifying nothing

was not Shakespeare's despair, but the despair belonging to a man who had killed his king. We may be too confident. All we can know is that it is a magnificent statement of despair, and that Shakespeare, writing *Macbeth*, makes it the sentiment of a man who has killed his king. In all the tragedies, cynicism and pessimism are shown to be the inheritance of those who are corrupted by misery, as with Timon, or the property of villains, as with Iago and Edmund, or a temporary distortion which can be

remedied through the education of experience, as with Hamlet and Lear. Yet, in the case of Timon, Hamlet, Macbeth and Lear, the statements of pessimism, or absurdity, or despair, are so very strong, and ring so insistently, that we cannot 'explain them away' as Shakespeare's superb ventriloquism, allowing him to make a character speak what he himself did not feel. They are the facts which make the writing of tragedy necessary, the defeat of the mind which makes the mind fight back to control its enemy in the theatre-image of life. In *Macbeth* the control is the control of orthodox Christian tragedy; in *Othello* and *King Lear* the control is more original.

Troilus and Cressida, in which there is no sense in the drift of events, answers *Hamlet*, in which a human action becomes the will of heaven. *All's Well* and *Measure for Measure*, in which a Christian movement of protection and redemption is attempted, answer *Troilus and Cressida*. *Othello* answers both *All's Well* and *Measure*, and *Troilus and Cressida*. It answers *Troilus and Cressida* in the person of Desdemona and her love for Othello: in asserting the existence of a woman's chastity and fidelity. It answers *All's Well* and *Measure for Measure* in a more sombre way. Those two plays are not able to make the salvation of the corrupt artistically convincing. Whatever Shakespeare's 'views' may be, he cannot as a playwright make the saint cure the devil in man. *Othello* is only too frightening a demonstration that he can do the opposite and show the devil corrupting innocence.

Desdemona is a woman who quickens one's imagination by her display of what it may mean to be a human being. Her marriage to Othello is a great imaginative act of independence and courage. When one thinks of the nineteenth-century novelist's ironic treatment of a woman's marriage as an attempt to soar above the unlovely restrictions of the life she is expected to live, in Dorothea Brooke, or Isabel Archer, one can only be sorry for the mistrust of their creators.

Everyone in the play fails to understand her, and fails her: her father, Iago, and, worst of all, Othello, whose misinterpretation of her 'appetite' is the cruellest thing in a bitter play. All that

Brabantio can recognize in the marriage is its strangeness; the only explanation he can find for his daughter's marrying a Moor is witchcraft. Again and again he insists that there must have been 'chains of magic' to make 'nature so preposterously to err'. But it is shown that Desdemona was 'half the wooer'. In her great speech, 'That I did love the Moor to live with him', she talks of her 'downright violence'. She knows whom she loves, she knows why she loves; and because she loves, she has made a free, positive, defiant choice. Sex is in it, but it is not sex.

The quality of Desdemona's love is a challenge to Iago's philosophy, and her very existence a pain to his being. Iago is the opposite of Thersites, who wanted women to be chaste, and was bitter because they weren't. He creates Desdemona in his words as he would have her in her nature. From the very first, he delights to distribute images of her sensuality.

> Even now, now, very now, an old black ram
> Is tupping your white ewe.

To keep Roderigo dangling, he assures him that Desdemona will tire of her man. Love is only 'a lust of the blood and a permission of the will'; 'She must change for youth. When she is sated with his body, she will find the error of her choice' (I, iii). 'When the blood is made dull with the act of sport, there should be, again to inflame it and to give satiety a fresh appetite, loveliness in favour, sympathy in years, manners and beauties, all which the Moor is defective in.' To Roderigo's 'She's full of most blest condition', Iago replies, 'Blest fig's-end! The wine she drinks is made of grapes. If she had been blest, she would never have loved the Moor. Blest pudding!' (II, i).

Iago does not believe all this; Desdemona *is* different. He knows that she loves the Moor because she is blest. He knows it, and he will not accept it. In the long scene of jesting with Desdemona while they wait at the quay (II, i) he pretends to be a bluff, good-humoured cynic about women. It is a clever mask, for his bantering refusal to accept 'a deserving woman indeed' is really a very sincere refusal. Iago's attempt to make Cassio agree that Desdemona is 'full of game' (II, iii, 16–25) may be a part of

his schemes, but it is also an attempt to win a convert to his ideology.

In spite of all Iago's immense intelligence, energy, and power to manipulate others, he is the most insecure of men. He is filled with the paranoiac's suspicion that others are always getting the better of him – Cassio in his professional life, Othello in his domestic life. The happiness of others is loathsome to him, and the 'daily beauty' of a life a perpetual offence. He is a man compact of jealousy, and he will destroy whatever is superior to his own ugliness of spirit.

Nothing offends him more than the purity of Desdemona. The war is between Iago and Desdemona; the destruction of Othello is the major battle in the war. Desdemona will not be what he will have all women to be – easy and licentious, governed by the thermostat of desire. Iago wants all humanity to be corruptible, so that he may see them corrupt. He can safely despise what he can easily bend: and what is bent can be no challenge to his own crookedness: he does not want mankind to be admirable. (So the temperate Cassio is made drunk: it is the kind of humiliation Iago loves.) Iago knows that Desdemona is incorruptible. She will not be reduced into the common weakness of *varium et mutabile* which he pretends to Roderigo is her real nature. If she will not come down to the only level of humanity which he can recognize and tolerate, he will so manage things that she will be treated as if she *were* corrupt – by her own husband.

Iago's soliloquy in II, iii makes it very clear where his true enemy is and what the shape of her defeat will be. His images distinguish between Desdemona and Othello. She is a free spirit; he is dependent (332–9). Then, when he has arranged it that this generous woman, 'as fruitful as the free elements', pleads to Othello on Cassio's behalf –

> I'll pour this pestilence into his ear,
> That she repeals him for her body's lust.
> And by how much she strives to do him good,
> She shall undo her credit with the Moor.
> So will I turn her virtue into pitch,
> And out of her own goodness make the net
> That shall enmesh them all.   (*II, iii, 347–53*)

'Turn her virtue into pitch'; it is the direct antithesis of the labours of Helena and the Duke of Vienna, who strove to turn evil intentions into good results. If Desdemona's goodness is unassailable, the corruption of others may make her destroy herself through her practice of goodness.

The triumph of Iago over Othello is a triumph over a lesser creature than Desdemona. To call the nobility of the 'early' Othello into question is perversity: it makes Desdemona cheap and the play meaningless. But the fact that he can allow suspicion of Desdemona to enter his mind, however diabolic the ingenuity of Iago may be, argues his love as simply not on her level. He is innocent in one sense; she in another and greater. Neither of them 'knows the world', but the ocean of difference in the quality of their ignorance can be seen if we set two passages against each other.

> *Iago:* In Venice they do let Heaven see the pranks
> They dare not show their husbands. Their best
> conscience
> Is not to leave't undone, but keep't unknown.
> *Othello:* Dost thou say so?   (*III, iii, 206–9*)

> *Desdemona:* Dost thou in conscience think – tell me, Emilia –
> That there be women do abuse their husbands
> In such gross kind?   (*IV, iii, 60–2*)

The failure of Othello to understand what Iago knows, the total difference of Desdemona from the women of Venice, is a kind of murder committed long before the bedroom scene. The crime is not that Othello should suspect his wife on insufficient evidence, but that he should class her with those who might be suspected. It is perhaps no more than a hair-line crack, but it is enough for Iago to work on.

At the end of the play Othello knows what he has done, and knows the quality of what he has lost. Whether or not his suicide is, literally, a damnable act, it is clear enough that before this he sees himself as one who has been betrayed by diabolic agency into doing a deed that will send him to hell. And yet *Othello*, if it is considered as a play of damnation, is very unlike *Macbeth*. It does not seem to place the action against a religious cosmos, in which heaven balances hell, let alone over-balances it. The hero has been corrupted, the innocent heroine murdered. In the end the villain is discovered, and is taken off to his punishment. The hero learns the truth, recognizes his guilt and (as he no doubt sees it) punishes himself with death. There seems to me to be a very fierce refusal to allow into this play any possible 'consolation'. To know what one has done, to be aware that one has been corrupted into throwing away the pearl richer than all one's tribe, is the utmost that is granted. There is nothing whatsoever that can be said to soften the betrayal and murder of Desdemona. *Othello* is a much more terrible play than *Troilus and Cressida*. One can deny the premisses in the latter play: one can say it doesn't try to investigate the possibilities of nobility and chastity. But nobility and chastity exist in *Othello*, and they collapse under a savage, willed destruction which *Troilus and Cressida* scarcely contemplates. Neither play leaves anything to be thankful for, but there is more to regret the loss of at the end of *Othello*. No play in the canon leaves one with such a sense of bafflement and helplessness as *Othello*.

> Will you, I pray, demand that demi-devil
> Why he hath thus ensnared my soul and body?

> Demand me nothing. What you know, you know.
> From this time forth I never will speak word.

What we know, we know. We know there is virtue of an extraordinary kind, and malice of an extraordinary kind, and that the malice turns the virtue into pitch. A man is tricked into misinterpreting innocence and purity, he becomes a murderer and kills himself when he realizes what he has done.

What seems to be so remarkable about *Othello* is that it makes its stark refusal to turn in any direction of comfort while maintaining a wonderful coherence and unity of form. If it had been a problem for Shakespeare that formal organization of a play forced on to the material a kind of pattern which might make life seem too reasonable altogether, the problem is solved in *Othello*. The artistic victory, however, is only a temporary victory. The single movement of corruption is magnificently achieved, but it is only a single movement. The play highlights the one brutal movement of the ruin of nobility and ends abruptly before anyone can talk of hope. It excludes as much as *As You Like It* excludes: it is a 'partial' play. With *King Lear* Shakespeare attempts the 'inclusive' play which one feels he was waiting all his life to write. It is certainly his most ambitious play. In its huge orchestration, it is always threatening to go beyond the powers of any stage or any actors – Elizabethan or otherwise. Yet at the same time it is one of the most 'theatrical' of his plays. 'All thought becomes an image'. Everything is presented to ears and eyes: the storm, the concourse of madmen, the blinding of Gloucester, the meeting of mad king and blind duke. Above all, passion itself, perhaps a blend of anger, self-pity, need, pomposity, tenderness, can be realized within a single speech. An actor has within a dozen lines the very fluctuations and contradictions that make personality. There are not so many plays in which we can find as we constantly find in Lear's speeches the *composite* quality of always-developing personality. A character may change his mind – as Hamlet will do in a soliloquy – or he may in successive speeches give us a rapid view of the different pressures and tensions within him, as Othello does when attacked by Iago's insinuations. But compare with these the kind of nakedness of mind one gets in such speeches as Lear's 'I prithee, daughter, do not make me mad' in Act II, scene iv.

This 'huge orchestration' of *Lear* spreads the action wide until it seems to involve the whole universe. The sub-plot gives a generalizing force to the main plot. By means of images, invocations, choric speeches, general reflections, the whole principle of human existence and continuance is brought on to the stage and into the story of Lear and his daughters. But this play, theatrically so daring and so universal in its reference, is yet simple in its idea. The good are good and the bad are bad, and in between them ranges Lear, tragically mistaken and faulty, but, 'more sinned against than sinning', pulled into his proper fold. The values of the play are quite steadfast under the raid of viciousness. We know where we are at any time, and can at any time take the bearing of any character against the firm traditional concepts of good and evil. It is not so in what are perhaps subtler plays, *Hamlet* and *Othello*. The idea of redemption is not a complicated idea (though the Epistle to the Romans is difficult reading). But it is hard to make a convincing artistic demonstration of redemption. Hence the paradox: Shakespeare brings all his resources together to give life to what is not in the least enigmatic.

For the plan of the play, Shakespeare returned to the three-part movement of the festive comedy which he had not touched for five years or more. We begin with the sundering of family and the separation of lovers (father and daughter): we have the central stage of bewilderment in the wild place, where identities are confused and persons are changed: we have the later stage of reunion and peace, when father and daughter are at one. But of course we have too the fourth stage, when the promise of the happy ending is crushed by Edmund's forgetfulness and Cordelia's death. The incorporation of the comedy structure is of very great importance. It shows Shakespeare working at the same problem that occupied him in *All's Well* and *Measure for Measure*: blending tragedy and comedy and trying to use the form of comedy as a vehicle for the idea of saving and cure. The solution is radically different. In the tragicomedies the old structure of festive comedy was discarded, and everything was made to depend upon the too-elaborate movement towards a surprise happy-ending. Now the happy ending is discarded and the tripartite structure resumed.

There is very little disagreement about 'what happens' in *Lear*, and a very rapid move towards the end will save repeating what everyone knows. The storm is a complex symbol. It is the surge of evil, which, with the shutting out of Lear and then the seeking of his death, is now deepening and spreading rapidly. It shows the futility of Lear's struggle with the universe, as at one moment he tries to fight the elements and at the next asks the storm to help him to destroy mankind. It is his punishment, as he recognizes. And it is his teacher. The thunder and the rain are the 'dreadful summoners' who teach him his own infirmity, who make his old assumptions about himself and his society vanish, and who reveal to him the true enemies of the gods. As his mind gives, he relinquishes the beliefs about what made him the man he was – position, dignity, obedience, awe, possessions – and accepts others based on the painful acquaintance with 'unaccommodated man'. In self-recognition, he recognizes other men, changing completely a valuation of worth based on outsides, and accepting the equal sinfulness of all – judge and vagabond: all 'offend', or, as he puts it, 'none does offend':

> None does offend, none, I say none, I'll able 'em.
> Take that of me, my friend, who have the power
> To seal the accuser's lips.   (*IV, vi, 170-2*)

As he awakens out of the deep restoring sleep, in fresh garments and to the sound of music, finding at his side the true object of love which he had rejected, Cordelia, we have a possible ending for the play. The three-fold movement is complete in this moving scene of reintegration.

> — Do not laugh at me,
> For, as I am a man, I think this lady
> To be my child Cordelia.
>   — And so I am, I am.
> — Be your tears wet? Yes, faith. I pray weep not.

>   You must bear with me.
> Pray you now, forget and forgive. I am old and foolish.
>   (*IV, vii, 68-71, 83-4*)

But this point of rest is not a point of rest for the world they live in. There is a momentum which cannot be stayed by the reconciliation of the main characters, as it can be in comedy. A war is in train, a battle is lost, and Lear and Cordelia are taken prisoner. The suggestion is now that if a world in movement cannot be arrested when individuals find their own peace, it can be rejected.

>   Come, let's away to prison.
> We two alone will sing like birds i' the cage.
> When thou dost ask me blessing, I'll kneel down
> And ask of thee forgiveness. So we'll live,
> And pray, and sing, and tell old tales, and laugh

At gilded butterflies, and hear poor rogues
Talk of court news. And we'll talk with them too,
Who loses and who wins, who's in, who's out,
And take upon's the mystery of things
As if we were God's spies. And we'll wear out,
In a walled prison, packs and sects of great ones
That ebb and flow by the moon. . . .
Upon such sacrifices, my Cordelia,
The gods themselves throw incense. Have I caught thee?
He that parts us shall bring a brand from Heaven,
And fire us hence like foxes.   (*V, iii, 8–23*)

In the majesty of this mood, there is a second 'possible ending'. The meaning of life has been found: it is in the union of two people between whom there is love without sex. The love exists in the recognition of unworthiness and the need for mutual forgiveness. They can take upon themselves the inner secret of all that the world displays, 'the mystery of things', and the knowledge they have, teaching them to despise the writhings of power and place, is a divine knowledge. The willingness to surrender physically to what physical privation is imposed on the two of them, while holding firm to each other is itself a 'sacrifice', a blest offering of themselves to a sphere higher than the world.

There is nothing in Shakespeare higher than this moment. It is the most 'real' of all the happy endings, since it shirks nothing and affirms everything. It makes sense of the world while denying nothing of the unpleasantness that is in the world. It brings together in a single dramatic image the exhilaration of the union of lovers and the oppression and malice which work against their happiness. An old and feeble father and his daughter going willingly to prison is the gesture which ties together *Love's Labour's Lost*, *Romeo and Juliet* and *As You Like It*.

Yet the killing of Cordelia – so markedly 'put in' by Shakespeare – is an act which must transform everything we feel about Lear's idea of sacrifice. A repentant and dying Edmund cancels too late the sentence he had commissioned in his villainy. Lear, who left the stage going with Cordelia in such strange joy to prison, enters again with Cordelia dead in his arms. He had said 'he that parts us shall bring a brand from Heaven'. It is a kind of

accident that parts them; it is not happy to think that Edmund's
delay is a brand from heaven. Lear had understood his happiness
as the sharing of his life with Cordelia. And Cordelia is brutally
taken away from him.

> Thou'lt come no more,
> Never, never, never, never, never!

It is improper to say that the union is continued in an after-life
and that therefore the bitterness of the loss is sweetened. If Shakespeare had wished to say this, he could have said it. Lear's death
is described simply as a release from his sufferings 'upon the rack
of this tough world'. Othello may have visions of an after life,
but in *Lear* it seems that spiritual states are conceived of by the
hero in terms of alterations in *mortal* existence; the divine is
known in the fructification of human life; and if this fruitfulness
is found not in solitude but in the relation between two persons,
then the death of one can take away the meaning that was newly-
found. The death of Lear is not shown as a release *to* happiness,
but a release *from* unbearable distress: a kind of euthanasia at a
moment when perhaps for a fleeting second he thinks Cordelia
is not dead.[48] Many years ago Wilson Knight wrote very forcibly
that the death of Cordelia was the 'most horrible of all the horrible
incongruities' in the play. 'Now we think that golden love was
but an oasis in a desert pilgrimage: no continuing city. . . Wherein
shall we seek our revelation – in that deathless dream of love, or
in this death?'[49] We shall certainly seek it in both: Shakespeare
has insisted on recording both revelations within the space of a
single scene.

Just so, in the Sonnets, the 'revelation' of being trapped by lust
accompanies the 'revelation' of release in love through mutual
forgiveness; accompanies it and, being placed last, always challenges it. What is found in *King Lear* is the idea of a relationship, won after much trial, which makes sense of human confusion and against this is placed the fact of a brutal death.
And these are the twin peaks which perpetually confront one
another.

The death of Cordelia is to be remembered throughout the
last plays, *Pericles, Cymbeline, The Winter's Tale, The Tempest.*

The Romances have really been written in *King Lear*, and the peace of their moving conclusions, in which daughter and wife are restored to the father, is confronted and threatened by the 'horrible incongruity' of a sudden and violent death.

Timon of Athens is the one play among the tragedies which shows Shakespeare struggling with the problem of form as he seems to have struggled in *All's Well* and *Measure for Measure*. I take it that it is an unfinished play. There are good arguments for accepting the usual later date, about 1607-8; the supple and compressed verse, the use of a masque, the novelty of a more primitive kind of dramatic presentation, may argue that it stands at the threshold of the last plays. If the late date is correct, then the presence in the play of themes which are treated in *Lear*, *Coriolanus* and *Antony and Cleopatra* would be evidence that Shakespeare gave up the play because he found that he was repeating himself. The similarities in theme between *Timon* and these three other tragedies are obvious. Like Lear, Timon inveighs against ingratitude and goes, scarcely sane, to a wild place where his curses become generalized anathemata of human kind and human continuance. The Coriolanus-theme of banishment by an ungrateful city, and the leading of an army in revenge against that city, is prominent in the Alcibiades-plot. And, as in *Antony and Cleopatra*, we have a story of a man of magnificent generosity declining in a world of pettier people.

These 'repetitions', however, may well be anticipations. Shakespeare may have been working on *Timon* before he wrote *King Lear*. He may have found his dramatic structure intractable; it is certainly very rigid.[50] Essentially, it consists of two movements: in the first, Timon is at the centre distributing munificence; in the second Timon is at the centre distributing curses. Is it not very likely that Shakespeare simply gave the play up, and chose to develop its themes in different plays? Whatever the extent of Shakespeare's dissatisfaction, we ought to be grateful for the publishing squabble which held up the printing of *Troilus and Cressida* in the First Folio and caused the manuscript *Timon* to be fished out of some chest and printed in its place. We should have

lost a great deal if it had not been rescued. We should not have
known, for example, of Shakespeare's power to write satirical
merchant comedy in a style which only Middleton can equal.
The scenes in which one after another Timon's beneficiaries
find excuses for not helping him in his need (the first three
scenes of Act III) are brilliant, and have no parallel elsewhere in
Shakespeare.

We should have lost Shakespeare's attack on his own profession. The Poet and the Painter are as bad as any who flatter
Timon for what he has to give, both in his heyday and in his
exile. In the first scene, they show themselves as men who know
and sigh over the slippery turns of Fortune's bill, and the Poet has
a work to present to Timon which might seem to be a warning
against betrayal. But Apemantus knows why they feign Timon
a worthy fellow. Their sycophantism is made worse by their self-
righteousness:

> 'When we for recompense have praised the vile,
> It stains the glory in that happy verse
> Which aptly sings the good.'   (*I, i, 14-16*)

This is apparently the beginning of the Poet's piece for Timon.
He can talk very well of dependants who will not help the favour-
ite of Fortune once he is going downhill, 'not one accompanying
his declining foot'. Yet what do the Poet and Painter do when he
is in distress but seek him out because they hear he has found gold?

> You shall see him a palm in Athens again, and flourish with the
> highest. Therefore 'tis not amiss we tender our loves to him in
> this supposed distress of his.   (*V, i, 11-14*)

> Nay, let's seek him.
> Then do we sin against our own estate
> When we may profit meet, and come too late.
>   (*V, i, 39-41*)

The Poet is ready to promise him the gift of a poem which will
be 'a personating of himself, a satire against the softness of pros-
perity'; but Timon overhears them so that their headshaking over

the ingratitude of men has a poor effect on him. The collection of specimens of the corruptibility of man in *Timon* is not large, and by including artists Shakespeare seems to mount a special attack against them. Does he include himself among those who tend to write whatever they think will melt a patron into disbursing? If Shakespeare excludes himself, he immediately becomes something like the pharisaical poet scorning the faults of others whom he portrays in the first scene. If he excludes himself, he becomes like the Timon of the last scenes, supposedly immune from the frailty of his kind, inveighing against the vices of others. The 'lesson' of *Timon* is of the barrenness of the wholesale condemnation of others; it travels part of the way along the *Lear* road, which teaches that all men are sinful – 'None does offend, none, I say none.' It is very hard to think that the man who wrote *Timon* and *Lear* could create the Poet and the Painter without feeling that he shared their flexibility. In *A Midsummer Night's Dream*, Shakespeare, in Theseus, brings in the suggestion that art constructs what mankind needs –

> – if it would but apprehend some joy,
> It comprehends some bringer of that joy.

In *Timon of Athens*, in his own person, Shakespeare suggests that highly moral art may owe its existence to the very material needs of the poet. The creating of the Poet adds to what we have already seen of Shakespeare's cold scrutiny of the nature of art.

Finally, the preservation of the unfinished *Timon* enables us to see very clearly the formation of a certain kind of symbolic writing which is to dominate the Romances. Yeats was fascinated by the death of Timon;[51] he called the ordering of the tomb one of the 'great moments' in Shakespeare.

> Lie where the light foam of the sea may beat
> Thy gravestone daily.

He quoted a passage in 'The Symbolism of Poetry':

> Timon hath made his everlasting mansion
> Upon the beached verge of the salt flood,
> Who once a day with his embossed froth
> The turbulent surge shall cover.

(The effect of the epitaph itself on Yeats is plain enough:

> 'Here lie I, Timon, who alive all living men did hate.
> Pass by and curse thy fill, but pass and stay not here thy gait.')

The image of Timon 'entombed upon the very hem o' the sea' is evocative indeed. The lines which Yeats quoted form a magnificent end to a magnificent last tirade (beginning at V, i, 185).

> My long sickness
> Of health and living now begins to mend,
> And nothing brings me all things.

He talks of all the pain which 'nature's fragile vessel doth sustain In life's uncertain voyage' and recommends all Athenians who wish 'to stop affliction' to come to his tree – and hang themselves. So it is the peace of death the sea stands for; the tide daily washes clean the strand, enveloping the tomb: mortality stands at the edge of a wide sea; from the accidents of life and individuality man is absorbed into 'this great vast' as Pericles calls it.

But the sea is not fused into the story as it is in *Pericles*. It is an addendum, and it makes us think about its meaning. The great power of the symbolism of the last plays is that it is not in the least allegorical. It requires no key to tell us 'what the sea stands for'. The sea, the shipwrecks, the jewels, the music, the flowers, virginity, the partings and reunions are fully self-subsistent. They are the story itself, and they need no interpretation to achieve their effect. They 'stand for' nothing but themselves. But they do not end with themselves; they perpetually reach out from the particular to the universal. Even Coleridge's great statement about symbolism does not fully cover the Shakespearian achievement. A symbol, he wrote 'always partakes of the reality which it renders intelligible: and while it enunciates the whole, abides itself as a living part in that unity of which it is the representative'.[52] Near though this comes to what Shakespeare does in the Romances, it suggests too much a schematic relationship between a knowable universal reality (macrocosm) and the vivid symbolic representation (microcosm). The relationship between particular and universal in Shakespeare is much more mysterious.

The value of the symbolism in *Timon* is that it is rough and ready, inchoate; we can see Shakespeare at work. We can register the success of the Romances against the unfinished quality of *Timon*. The gold itself, discovered by Timon as he digs for roots, is rough and ready symbolism. Financially ruined, he suddenly finds lumps of that which would restore him. But in the new understanding, it is not a restorative, but poison; and he will distribute it to hasten the self-destruction of mankind. The 'point' of the insidious rotting of natural pieties by the commercial relationship of man to man is too heavily made.

The most striking of all the symbolism in *Timon*, however, is the sudden opportunism at the end which turns Athens into a symbolic City of Man of medieval kind. It becomes the walled city of iniquity. Timon had urged Alcibiades to undertake the city's destruction:

> Be as a planetary plague, when Jove
> Will o'er some high-viced city hang his poison
> In the sick air; let not thy sword skip one.
>
> *(IV, iii, 110–12)*

Now he approaches with his army.

> Sound to this coward and lascivious town
> Our terrible approach. *(V, iv, 1–2)*

The Senators plead for mercy: pleading for mankind against 'the promised end'. The city is older and greater than those sinful inhabitants who have offended (22–6); in any case 'all have not offended'; 'cull the infected forth, But kill not all together' (35, 43–4). The pleading converts Alcibiades: he promises to punish only the known criminals and to show mercy to the rest: 'I will use the olive with my sword'. It is during this final scene of relenting that the news of Timon's death comes and his epitaph is read. Alcibiades interprets Timon's 'rich conceit' (the imaginative idea) of the sea-washed tomb as his final pity for the sins Timon would not forgive when alive.

> Though thou abhor'dst in us our human griefs
> . . . yet rich conceit
> Taught thee to make vast Neptune weep for aye
> On thy low grave, on faults forgiven. *(V, iv, 75, 77–9)*

The phrase 'human griefs' for all that Timon has inveighed against is very powerful. Alcibiades is exceptionally charitable both to mankind and to Timon's spirit, but the melting mood in the ending could not be better conveyed. (Wilson Knight, in his impassioned but striking essay on *Timon* in *The Wheel of Fire* believed that the 'faults forgiven' were Timon's faults, but it can hardly be so.)

The final city-scene is in a very different key from the rest of the play; it strongly suggests a leap towards the dramatic method of the Romances. In *Pericles* there is the City of Incest, Antiochus, and the famine-stricken City of Vanity, Tharsus, and in *The Tempest* the city becomes an island. The theme of relenting of one's destructive vengeance is repeated at the ending of *The Tempest*. What is contained within the city, as well as its fate, is important. Timon's revolting pictures of lechery, sexual delinquency and venereal disease may arise from an infected mind. But the idea of men and women destroying themselves by lust links up with other plays more than does the idea of the destructive power of the 'cash-nexus', which is *Timon*'s special feature. The *cupiditas* which is the root of all evil is carnal more than it is pecuniary. *King Lear* plays in an astonishing way with the idea of sexual intercourse being the root cause of the sufferings of both Gloucester and Lear; the damage which libidinous mankind inflicts on itself is the main datum on which the Romances are built, and the main effort is to find the Desdemona-figure who is immune from the self-destroying curse of humankind.

attention to the romance on which it is based (Apollonius of Tyre). The narrative structure is carefully preserved by the choruses of old Gower who at intervals tells so much of the story, then asks the audience to witness one piece of it in dumb-show, and see another in full theatre.

> The Lady shrieks and well-a-near
> Does fall in travail with her fear;
> And what ensues in this fell storm
> Shall for itself itself perform.
> I nill relate, action may
> Conveniently the rest convey.   (*III, Prol. 51–6*)

A tale, an old tale, and a tale full of wonders; *Pericles* asks not for belief but for disbelief; it asks the audience to enjoy it as make-believe and not to mistake it for an image of what has been or what might be. It is simply 'a story'. Pericles solves a famous riddle, flees for his life, is shipwrecked, wins a tournament and a fair lady, and loses his wife at sea; her body is washed ashore and she is brought back to life; his daughter is believed murdered, but is actually captured by pirates; she escapes from a brothel, and is by strange coincidence united with her father; a goddess directs them to Ephesus, and there Pericles discovers his long-lost wife.

Pericles plays with the beauty or the pathos of the moments of the tale which it dramatizes. It has little interest in their relation one to another except in their being parts of the life of Pericles. The uncouth fishermen who succour the shipwrecked Pericles are in the play only to show the warmth of kindness as a contrast to the previous coldness of both humanity and the elements. The feast at which Thaisa and Pericles fall in love, the resuscitation of the 'dead' Thaisa, the appearance of Diana to Pericles 'in a vision' are moments of beauty or power in themselves. It is a little different with the two major scenes of the play, showing Marina in the brothel and the reunion of Marina and Pericles, because for these we need to be involved in what Marina and Pericles are and in pity for what has befallen them. Nevertheless we are never involved with them as we are with Lear and Cordelia; the inhabitants of the brothel just come into the story and disappear again like the fishermen (the parts were presumably doubled) and father

10

Last Plays

In his mid forties, Shakespeare turned away from tragedy to write the group of plays now generally called his Romances: *Pericles, Cymbeline, The Winter's Tale, The Tempest.* The suddenness of the break and the strangeness of the plays have seemed to critics to demand some special kind of explanation, which they have found in the condition of Shakespeare's soul, in the pressure of fashionable drama, in the conditions of the theatre, in a preoccupation with myth or eschatology, in a weariness with writing plays.[53] There seems to be a measure of truth in almost all the explanations. It is not with any attempt at flippancy, however, that one says that Shakespeare wrote these plays because he wanted to.

An obstacle to our getting a clear view of the Romances is our uncertainty about *Pericles, Prince of Tyre*, which has come down to us in a maimed text. Although there are not three consecutive lines of verse in the whole play which are indisputably Shakespeare's, and though the first half of the play is so wretchedly written that few people can believe that Shakespeare had more than a minimal responsibility for it, I cling to the possibility that there once existed an entire Pericles-play of Shakespeare's invention which two men, with differing degrees of infidelity and illiteracy, 'reconstructed' in order to provide a text for a rival company.[54] Whether the original was wholly Shakespeare's or not, the critic of the play has to be an archaeologist inferring the nature of a building from its ruins.

Pericles was 'a mouldy tale' to Ben Jonson, and the noun is right whatever we think of the adjective. Pericles is unashamedly a tale, a narrative of wanderings, love and adventure which calls

K

and daughter come together accidentally after a separation that was in the beginning scarcely forced on them. Whether all the events are likely to happen in the nature of things or in the nature of the story does not really matter. They are events in the life story of a romance-hero. They have their own force – a force which is undeniable, as every stage-production testifies. The force is elemental. It is built on the strength of the sea, of famine, of marriage, of childbirth, of bereavement, of a girl threatened with rape, a father and daughter reunited.

Parts of the evil in the play are simply 'points to be noted'. The incest which Pericles discovers at Antioch, the tyranny of Antiochus, the murderous envy of Dionyza, are items direct from stock. Not so the brothel at Mytilene. Marina, a figure of youth, innocence, beauty and spirit, is more carefully characterized than anyone else in the play. She stands unprotected amidst the threatenings and gross jests of the pandar, the bawd and Boult, who go about preparing their new prize to entertain their disease ridden customers. The extremes of the world meet. It is an attempted rape upon innocence and innocence wins through. She shames the clients, and converts the Governor himself, Lysimachus, who wanders into the brothel cheerfully seeking his pleasure.[55] The clash between virgin innocence and the worst of the slaves of Venus, with their defeat, is the strongest thing in the play, and, together with the reunion of father and daughter, the most important link between *Pericles* and the other romances.

There is a similarity in form between *Pericles* and *The Winter's Tale* in that the latter also ostentatiously covers a long period of time, though the many narrative links by Gower are reduced to the single speech by Time.

> Impute it not a crime
> To me or my swift passage that I slide
> O'er sixteen years and leave the growth untried
> Of that wide gap. (*IV, i, 4–7*)

But essentially *The Winter's Tale* belongs not with *Pericles* but with *The Tempest*. It uses the three-stage structure of comedy which surely has its fulfilment in *The Tempest*. In *The Winter's Tale* we are moved from diseased court to pastoral sheep-farm where disguise and unknown identity cause their confusions, then back again to a court refreshed with the marriage of young lovers and the reunion of a broken family. *The Tempest* enlarges the 'central area' of confusion until it occupies almost the whole play. In *The Tempest* the pattern of comedy initiated in *The Comedy of Errors* is completed. In none of the festive comedies has the enchantment, with its bewilderment and confusion, been so extravagant, in none has the sense of evil been so grave, in none has the quality of richness in the promise of the ending been so great. *The Tempest* takes its place in a whole genre of island literature, which includes such works as *Utopia, Robinson Crusoe, Gulliver's Travels, Victory, Riders to the Sea, The Man Who Loved Islands, Lord of the Flies*. The island nearly always suggests either an isolated retreat from the world, or else the world (or mortal life) itself; there is therefore a very great temptation to take *The Tempest* as an allegory of the whole of life. The temptation must for a while be resisted. The play must be seen as a particular story, flaunting its improbability like *Pericles* and having an effect on us differing in degree and not in kind from the effect of *Comedy of Errors* and *As You Like It*. It is a particular, unrealistic story, celebrating the overcoming of evil, the triumph of love, the victory over time and supersession, and affecting us with the pleasure that comedy of this kind has always given. Prospero's masque to celebrate the betrothal of his daughter with the son of his old enemy is a thing of immense beauty:

> Juno: Honour, riches, marriage-blessing,
> Long continuance and increasing,
> Hourly joys be still upon you!
> Juno sings her blessings on you.
> Ceres: Earth's increase, foison plenty,
> Barns and garners never empty,
> Vines with clustering bunches growing,
> Plants with goodly burden bowing:
> Spring come to you at the farthest
> In the very end of harvest!
> Scarcity and want shall shun you,
> Ceres' blessing so is on you.   (IV, i, 106–17)

Gonzalo's speeches combine the sense of earthly promise with divine blessing and reward and speak of the new harmony among the people of the play in terms of the recovery of the true self which would serve not only for every festive comedy but for *King Lear* too:

> Look down, you gods,
> And on this couple drop a blessed crown!
> For it is you that have chalked forth the way
> Which brought us hither. . . .
> Was Milan thrust from Milan, that his issue
> Should become kings of Naples? Oh, rejoice
> Beyond a common joy! and set it down
> With gold on lasting pillars. In one voyage
> Did Claribel her husband find at Tunis
> And Ferdinand, her brother, found a wife
> Where he himself was lost, Prospero his dukedom
> In a poor isle, and all of us ourselves
> When no man was his own.   (*V, i, 201–13*)

Shakespeare has written a comedy which is at the same time serious *and* light-hearted, improbable *and* immensely convincing. It is 'inclusive' of the real pain and evil in the world, yet the promise of the ending is not forced nor in any way ironic. Though Antonio is sullen and Caliban still to be reckoned with (he says he will 'seek for grace'), there is no Jaques to go back to the abandoned cave, no feeling, as in *Love's Labour's Lost*, that a whole world is ignored in a happy ending of lover's meetings, no sense (as in *Twelfth Night*) of anything less than full and mutual love between two persons in Miranda and Ferdinand.

And yet, *The Tempest* is a very far-fetched story, however fine its wholeness of mood and its sense of shirking nothing. How far can it be generalized? How far is it a myth usable as a formula to interpret our own experience, as well as a ritual to encourage and invigorate us?

In *The Winter's Tale*, though not in *The Tempest*, we are given things from time to time which seem to undermine rather than underprop the fiction. The play is about renewal, about restoring what was corrupt, through penitence, and through the new life abounding in the young lovers of the new generation, Perdita and Florizel. Like *The Tempest*, it makes much use of the *felix culpa* by which an evil intention brings about a good result. Leontes' attempt to kill his child leads to the union of the sundered families of Sicily and Bohemia. The union of kingdoms Gonzalo sees as something which God can produce from the evil of Prospero's banishment. There is a clear link here with the endeavour in *All's Well* and *Measure for Measure*, and where there is failure there, there is success here – though not complete. Shakespeare does not really attempt to show the salvation of the corrupt extended in time. The weight of *The Tempest* is elsewhere, and in *The Winter's Tale* Leontes does not go into the purgatorial wilderness. He repents as soon as the news of his son's death is brought to him, and the whole sense of renewal depends on what grows between Perdita and Florizel during his (unobserved) years of expiation.

Everything depends on these two. We feel it so strongly in all these four plays that 'everything depends' on the success with which the happiness, richness and innocence of youth and young love is drawn. Iachimo has got to be proved wrong about women, and the love between Posthumus and Imogen not only true but known by each other to be true (contrast *Othello*); the rough lust of Cloten has got to be defeated. The vision of woman *varium et mutabile* which was Hamlet's vision and the 'lesson' of *Troilus and Cressida* is shown as a diseased imagination in Leontes. Leontes is not an Iago in a narrow-eyed, pursed-lips 'realism' about women. He is like the dramatist in the grip of thoughts which would make him write *Hamlet* or *Troilus and Cressida*, thoughts which he later knows to be madness. He forces innocent people, his own wife and children, to live in this world of his own creating, and to suffer as though they were the whores and bastards his demon insists they are. He can see only corruption, and in seeing it, 'nothing is but what is not'. Hermione says, 'My life stands in the level of your dreams.' All lives, in fiction, stand in the level of the writer's dreams. If Leontes' vision of universal lechery and betrayal (see especially I, ii, 186–207) is made to be the vision of a deranged mind, what of the vision of goodness and promise?

One of the most curious passages in *The Winter's Tale* is Polixenes' rhapsody on the innocence of childhood friendship in the second scene. He speaks of himself and Leontes:

> We were, fair queen,
> Two lads that thought there was no more behind
> But such a day tomorrow as today,
> And to be boy eternal. . . .
> We were as twinned lambs that did frisk i'the sun,
> And bleat the one at the other. What we changed
> Was innocence for innocence; we knew not
> The doctrine of ill-doing, nor dreamed
> That any did. Had we pursued that life,
> And our weak spirits ne'er been higher reared
> With stronger blood, we should have answered Heaven
> Boldly 'Not guilty,' the imposition cleared
> Hereditary ours.   (I, ii, 62–75)

The jesting exchange with Hermione which follows enforces what has already been clearly implied – that the marriages of the two men are part of the access of guilt and of the departure of innocence.

> *Hermione:*   By this we gather
>   You have tripped since.
> *Polixenes:*   O my most sacred lady!
>   Temptations have since then been born to's. For
>   In those unfledged days was my wife a girl,
>   Your precious self had then not crossed the eyes
>   Of my young playfellow.
> *Hermione:*   Grace to boot!
>   Of this make no conclusion, lest you say
>   Your queen and I are devils!   (I, ii, 75–82)

Polixenes' remarks have a special ironic force in that he is almost immediately to learn how terribly, more terribly than ever he could have conceived, the innocence of his relations with Leontes has been darkened by 'stronger blood'. But his picture of 'the

darkening green' is much more than a prelude to Leontes' out-
burst, it is a statement which casts a shadow over the whole play
and, I believe, over all the last plays. Clifford Leech compared and
contrasted this exchange with the cynical attitude to grown love
in *The Two Noble Kinsmen*: I shall shortly follow up the comparison. Leech has also spoken about the puritanical treatment of
sex in the last plays;[56] this seems to me to be closely related to
Polixenes' nostalgia for childish innocence.

With his view of childhood, it is natural that Polixenes should
delight in sharing the life of his own child –

> He makes a July's day short as December,
> And with his varying childness cures in me
> Thoughts that would thick my blood. (*I, ii, 169–71*)

Leontes and his awful obsession apart, there is in *The Winter's Tale*
the notion of the need for renewal in manhood which so soon
grows tired and tainted. Pericles wonderfully addresses Marina:

> Oh, come hither,
> Thou that beget'st him that did thee beget!
> (*V, i, 194–5*)

When Leontes greets Florizel and Perdita, before he knows that
she is his daughter, he is filled with the idea of their reliving the
youth of his own generation (V, i, 123–37).

> Welcome hither,
> As is the spring to the earth.

Yet if this renewal is somehow achieved by the freshness and
fullness of the love between this young man and this girl, what
becomes of that suggestion that true innocence is lost with the
dawn of sexuality?

> Had we pursued that life,
> And our weak spirits ne'er been higher reared
> With stronger blood, we should have answered Heaven
> Boldly, 'Not guilty.'

The most perverse criticism cannot make the love shown between Florizel and Perdita anything less than a supreme drawing of what is spontaneous, full, ardent and rich; there is no alloy in it. But we notice Florizel's insistence on the purity of his affection:

> My desires
> Run not before mine honour, nor my lusts
> Burn hotter than my faith. (*IV, iv, 33–5*)

Perdita: But that your youth
And the true blood which peeps fairly through't,
Do plainly give you out an unstained shepherd,
With wisdom I might fear, my Doricles,
You wooed me the false way.
Florizel: I think you have
As little skill to fear as I have purpose
To put you to it. (*IV, iv, 147–53*)

Though the princely wooer of a shepherdess may well need to clear himself of aiming at a seduction, the emphasis on purity in a scene so fertile in its flower imagery is rather disconcerting. It seems to me that Shakespeare wants to hold the beauty of this moment. It is a moment of free and frank giving, the one to the other, of two beings who have met and fallen in love. Pursuit has not come into it. It is a moment of giving of faith, before the giving of their bodies. He arrests the beauty of this moment, because the green place of the sheep-shearing feast is a darkening green. The play with the seasons in the great fourth scene of the fourth act seems to suggest sunlight against a black horizon. Perdita wears not her own clothes but those of a spring goddess – 'No shepherdess, but Flora / Peering in April's front' (IV, iv, 2–3). The important and elaborate sheep-shearing feast is not, however, an April rite, but takes place in late June.[57] In *The Winter's Tale* it is very oddly pushed still further on to a time towards the end of summer:[58]

> – the year growing ancient
> Not yet on summer's death nor on the birth
> Of trembling winter. (*IV, iv, 79–81*)

It is surely important that such a point is made of Perdita's acting

the part of the spring goddess in the middle or late summer. She
is able to provide flowers for the old men. But she turns to
Florizel and wishes that she in truth had the flowers appropriate
for youth:

> Now, my fair'st friend,
> I would I had some flowers o' the spring that might
> Become your time of day – and yours, and yours,
> That wear upon your virgin branches yet
> Your maidenheads growing. O Proserpina,
> For the flowers now that frighted thou let'st fall
> From Dis's wagon!

Perdita now creates spring in her words, as she speaks of the
daffodils, primroses, violets dim and lilies of all kinds, but she is,
almost, distressed that she does not really have these flowers:

> Oh, these I lack
> To make you garlands of, and my sweet friend,
> To strew him o'er and o'er.   (*127–9*)

The sense of acting is strong upon her; she is almost swept from
the reality of her being to the reality of her imagination:

> Come, take your flowers.
> Methinks I play as I have seen them do
> In Whitsun pastorals. Sure this robe of mine
> Does change my disposition.   (*132–5*)

Winter is approaching, while Perdita acts the newness of spring's
glory. The strongest argument against taking Perdita as Proserpine, Hermione as Ceres, and the whole play as a re-enactment
of the spring fertility-myth, is that Perdita so pointedly speaks
of her non-identity with Proserpine.

In arresting the fertility of youth and love at a certain point,
Shakespeare has at the same time wished to suggest the inevitable
decay of whatever is fresh and new. If spring comes, can winter be
far behind? When Time enters as Chorus at the beginning of Act
IV, he is not only a device to bridge a long gap in the narrative

of the story: he is inexorable time, whose hand is upon Perdita and
Florizel.

> Let me pass
> The same I am, ere ancient'st order was,
> Or what is now receiv'd. I witness to
> The times that brought them in; *so shall I do*
> *To th' freshest things now reigning, and make stale*
> *The glistering of this present*, as my tale
> Now seems to it. (*IV, i, 9–15*)

The sadness which seems in this *winter's tale* to accompany the
sunlight of love and renewal is present also in the famous 'debate'
between Polixenes and Perdita on art and nature. It is Polixenes'
argument that it is necessary to take nature in hand by art to
improve nature: to graft fresh growth on rougher stock. Yet he
opposes in practice the marriage of his son to a peasant girl. It is
Perdita's argument that such art is unnatural and indeed meretricious: she is all for 'great creating nature'. Yet she herself is
dressed up in 'borrowed flaunts', queening it, and changing her
disposition by acting. Perdita's refusal to accept the 'art of grafting'
takes us further into the concept of the play. For the play itself is a
story of grafting; of reinvigorating the old stock by the freshness
of unsullied youth and love. And this story is the work of art, not
a report of what great creating nature has done. The uncertainty
in the debate leads to uncertainty on whether (dramatic) art is
the refinement or the distortion of nature, an uncertainty which
has been all along the subject of this study.

Perhaps the extreme theatricality of Hermione's restoration to
Leontes, as a statue coming to life, is in some measure a comment
in support of Perdita's view of things. The whole statue scene
(like the preservation of Hermione) is such a reckless piece of
improbability, its theatrical effectiveness so very uncertain, that
Shakespeare might seem to be insisting that art is not nature.

So it may be that the life of Florizel and Perdita, the repentance
of Leontes and the restoration of Hermione also stand in the level
of dreams. The vision of beauty and blessing and bounty at the
centre of the play *is* a vision, 'like an old play still' (V, ii, 62). It is
a jewel cut and polished by Shakespeare's art, and it is put in a
setting which girdles youth about with the threat of vanishing

innocence and time's decay. It is a moment of extreme beauty, taken out of time, and then lodged back into time.

To return, then, to the question of *The Tempest*; whether this, like *The Winter's Tale*, puts all its great power into displaying the beauty of what it acknowledges to be dream rather than substance.

Who is Prospero? He is the magician who uses his art for discipline, order and control. He has identified his enemies, and he has brought them within his power. Not only has he to subdue the malice of his peers, Antonio and Alonso, but to contain, and indeed employ, the brute force of savagery in Caliban. When all are held by him, he works to create a more blessed future in bringing Ferdinand and Miranda together, and seeing love grow between them.

> Fair encounter
> Of two most rare affections! Heavens rain grace
> On that which breeds between 'em!   (*III, i, 74–6*)

But this love too must be the subject of control. Miranda is, like Marina and Perdita, the image of innocent virginity. She is somehow to be moved to the rich promise of fertility (see the blessings of Ceres and Juno) without the 'contamination' which blots the relations between Claudio and Julietta in *Measure for Measure*. Continence is the right word. The ebullience of 'blood' in the Elizabethan sense is to be kept under if Prospero's magic is to work: it is as much a destructive element as the plotting of Antonio and Sebastian:

> If thou dost break her virgin knot before
> All sanctimonious ceremonies may
> With full and holy rite be ministered,
> No sweet aspersion shall the heavens let fall
> To make this contract grow; but barren hate,
> Sour-eyed disdain and discord shall bestrew
> The union of your bed with weeds so loathly
> That you shall hate it both.   (*IV, i, 15–22*)

Venus and her son are banished from the masque. Ceres has for-
sworn her company:

> Of her society
> Be not afraid. I met her deity
> Cutting the clouds towards Paphos, and her son
> Dove-drawn with her. Here thought they to have done
> Some wanton charm upon this man and maid,
> Whose vows are, that no bedright shall be paid
> Till Hymen's torch be lighted. But in vain;
> Mars's hot minion is returned again.   (*IV, i, 91–8*)

Venus here is neither Aphrodite Ourania, nor Aphrodite Pan-
demos, the goddesses of *amor divinus* and *amor humanus*, but a
Venus who is nearly the goddess of *amor ferinus* or *bestialis*.[59]

With his enemies controlled and (to some extent) cured, with
the natural and not pleasant vigour of man put into safe channels,
Prospero releases the spirit who has helped him to do this work,
and he enters on the inheritance which is more for others than
for himself. This victory is not more than half secured by force
and enchantment: until forgiveness begins to work it is negative
prevention only: without the energy of love in Ferdinand and
Miranda, there is nothing to build the future with.

Is it necessary to run away from the identification of Prospero
with Shakespeare? As J. W. Mackail remarked, 'The dramatist
has projected himself bodily into the drama.'[60] The whole endeavour of Prospero is so like the endeavour of the dramatist –
even down to putting characters into a situation in which they will
react, and then carefully heading them in a certain direction (the
court party isolated, the king put to sleep, the emergence of
Antonio's plot, its prevention; or, the bringing together of
Ferdinand and Miranda). Shakespeare has assembled all his characters, good, bad and indifferent, dissolved them into pastoral
typology. Bertram, the man who could not be redeemed, is
divided between Antonio and Caliban, finally irredeemable. Fal-
staff and Sir Toby Belch are there in the drunken sailors, comedy's
spirit of license finally rejected.

Prospero has organized and disciplined his world as the dramatist must do his in creating the ordered work of art. And he has
sent it off into the future, like a general releasing a pigeon with the

news of a victory, just as the writer of festive comedies ends his plays. The parallel between magician and dramatist is closest in the wedding masque, when Prospero is actually a producer who brings his actors on to give a show to delight and encourage his audience. This masque of blessing is as we have seen a quite indispensable moment in the progress of the play: it is an integral part of what Shakespeare is 'putting on'. Prospero suddenly dismisses his actors, remembering the more 'real' problem of Caliban's conspiracy. But he tells his audience of two not to be 'dismayed' by the disappearance of these revels 'into thin air'. They have disappeared as the whole pageant of life itself must disappear.[61]

> The great globe itself –
> Yea, all which it inherit – shall dissolve
> And, like this insubstantial pageant faded,
> Leave not a rack behind. We are such stuff
> As dreams are made on, and our little life
> Is rounded with a sleep.   (*IV, i, 153–8*)

There are three levels: the level of the play-within-the-play (the masque), the level of reality in which Prospero, who is a creature in a play, has to deal with Caliban, and the level of the audience's life. The first level vanishes, the second is within minutes of coming to an end, and the third is described as a dissolving dream. The reality of Prospero is not greater than the reality of the show his spirits performed; the reality of our lives (it is suggested) is not greater than the reality of Prospero.

It is at this moment that Shakespeare is 'the king himself'. 'They cannot touch me for coining' – for where lies the bedrock of reality which all his life he has been trying to draw into the compass of art? The bedrock is like the material of art, a 'baseless fabric'. Yeats quoted Vico as saying, 'We can know nothing that we have not made.'[62]

Shakespeare has worked the stuff of his experience into a creation whose precariousness – considered as a model of the world – he is only too anxious to remark on by pointing out here, as in *Pericles* and *The Winter's Tale*, that it is all a story, a rather far-fetched and preposterous story. The fragility seems to me most striking not so much in the ostentatious unlikelihood of magic or chance or coincidence as in the immensely beautiful pictures of youth and maiden, in love and espoused, but not together in full sexual relation. It is the moment of purity and promise which Prospero and Shakespeare work for: a moment of sunlight against a dark horizon to hold in contemplation. The argument that it is 'not life' has two answers: that it is as real a thing to contemplate this as to do anything else; and that if one looks elsewhere, like Bacon, for a true picture of 'reality' one has only fragments of suspicion, guesses and doubts, and the sense that 'we are such stuff as dreams are made on'.

The Tempest seems to be the supreme moment of balance when art can protest its own right to exist, immune from the sceptical challenge that it leaves out the evil of the world, and able to forge its own ritual of promise to encourage its audience without being accused of wishful thinking, since it pretends to be no more than a story. It is almost certainly the last complete play that Shakespeare wrote: its importance to him seems witnessed to by its being apparently his entire invention (there is no 'source' in the usual sense) and by the special place his fellows made for it at the beginning of his works in 1623. The identification with Prospero is completed if we go along with all those who have seen Prospero's relinquishing of his magic and release of Ariel as Shakespeare's abandonment of his craft. In many ways, there was nothing more for Shakespeare to do. Yet, at forty-eight, it was not necessarily with him as it was with Prospero, 'Every third thought shall be my grave.' He purchased the Blackfriars gatehouse – near the theatre – in 1613, and he collaborated with Fletcher in *Henry VIII*[63] and *The Two Noble Kinsmen*. It is in *The Two Noble Kinsmen*, when Shakespeare has quite clearly given up the responsibility of shaping an entire fiction which will be all the things he wanted every play of his to be, that one can see the pressure of doubt and dark uncertainty which tells us at the same time of the superb ordering power of *The Tempest*, and of the truth that it is not, and is not meant to be a picture of all that is real.

An image from the Romances which etches itself most sharply in the imagination is that of Marina in the brothel: purity surrounded but not contaminated by the lowest debasement that the sexual instinct achieves in society. Shakespeare does not again attempt so sharp a black-and-white distinction: Iachimo's fantasies and Cloten's lust concern a married woman, however chaste, and do not threaten Imogen in the way Marina is threatened. Hermione resists the contamination which Leontes' mind throws upon her, but again it is not the direct opposition of virginity and professional lechery. The attempted violation of Miranda by Caliban *is* of the same kind, but it is only referred to. We have seen that Shakespeare's attempt in *The Winter's Tale* and *The Tempest* is to try to disarm the disfiguring enemy, sexual desire, by transfiguring him. Without emasculating marriage, he creates his figures of virgin purity and lets their light surround the lovers' union, ostentatiously pushing out of the play the sexual side of that union. The exaltation of chaste maidenhood and the fear of the contamination of sexual relations are scarcely comprehensible, however orthodox and conventional they must have seemed a hundred years ago. It is important to see Shakespeare as something more than a man preoccupied with the problem of pre-marital sexual relations. Marina fighting off Boult and Lysimachus is an emblematic image of what was to Shakespeare the primeval warfare in the soul; Ferdinand and Miranda receiving the blessing and warning of Prospero bring us nearer to everyday life, but the sacramental idea seems on a plane beyond human wedding.

In *The Two Noble Kinsmen* the encounter of purity and sexuality is described in a stylized and 'conventional' presentation of two stages of life, and of the inevitable but deforming passage from one to another.[64]

Innocence is childhood and its impulsive affection, just as Polixenes had described it. Emilia, who repulses the idea of marriage, speaks of her girlhood with Flavina, who died when she was eleven.

I

> And she I sigh and spoke of were things innocent.
> Loved for we did, and like the elements
> That know not what nor why, yet do effect
> Rare issues by their operance, our souls
> Did so to one another: what she liked

Venus, the Venus who was kept out of the wedding masque of Ferdinand and Miranda, is the villain of the play. It is she (or quite simply, sexual desire) who takes Palamon and Arcite out of a non-sexual love as rich as that between Emilia and Flavina or Theseus and Pirithous and makes them enemies to each other and to themselves.

The centre of the play is Palamon's address to Venus, the goddess to whom he prays for victory (V, i, 77). Every additional tribute which Palamon pays to her might disgusts us the more. The older people get, the more ludicrous and grotesque becomes their behaviour as the almighty goddess twists them in her hands:

> Hail, sovereign queen of secrets, who hast power
> To call the fiercest tyrant from his rage
> And weep unto a girl . . .
>   . . . that canst make
> A cripple flourish with his crutch, and cure him
> Before Apollo . . .
>   . . . The poll'd bachelor –
> Whose youth like wanton boys through bonfires
> Have skipt thy flame – at seventy thou canst catch,
> And make him, to the scorn of his hoarse throat,
> Abuse young lays of love. What godlike power
> Hast thou not power upon ? . . .
>   . . . Take to thy grace
> Me, thy vowed soldier, who do bear thy yoke
> As 'twere a wreath of roses, yet is heavier
> Than lead itself, stings more than nettles . . .
>   . . . I knew a man
> Of eighty winters, this I told them, who
> A lass of fourteen brided: 'twas thy power
> To put life into dust; the agèd cramp
> Had screw'd his square foot round,
> The gout had knit his fingers into knots,
> Torturing convulsions from his globy eyes
> Had almost drawn their spheres, that what was life
> In him seemed torture; this anatomy
> Had by his young fair fere a boy, and I
> Believed it was his, for she swore it was,
> And who would not believe her? . . .

Was then of me approved; what not, condemned,
No more arraignment; the flower that I would pluc
And put between my breasts, O – then but beginnin
To swell about the blossom – she would long
Till she had such another, and commit it
To the like innocent cradle, where phoenix-like,
They died in perfume . . .

                    . . . this rehearsal –
Which every innocent wots well comes in
Like old importment's bastard – has this end,
That the true love 'tween maid and maid may be
More than in sex dividual.[65]   (*I, iii, 59–71, 78–82*

Emilia wants to live in the past, to try to hold on to this inn
cence, and not to marry; but even if the mere fact of adultho
being against her were not enough, the two young noble kin
men, Arcite and Palamon, fall in love with her and seek to w
her.

Emilia is only the most extreme – and poetic – of the chai
acters who realize the gravity of the move from the spontaneit
of innocence to adult sexual relations. Theseus and Hippolyt
move forward to their marriage trustfully enough, but the back-
ward glance is clearly there. In Theseus' life, Hippolyta comes in
to displace his friend Pirithous –

                    Their knot of love
Tied, weaved, entangled, with so true, so long,
And with a finger of so deep a cunning,
May be out-worn, never undone.   (*I, iii, 41–4*)

Of Hippolyta herself, the Amazonian huntress, we are told, with
strange imagery, that by marrying her Theseus

                    shrunk thee into
The bound thou wast o'erflowing, at once subduing
Thy force and thy affection.   (*I, i, 83–5*)

The friendship of Palamon and Arcite is everything in their lives
and their love for Emilia destroys it.

O thou that from eleven to ninety reign'st
In mortal bosoms, whose chase is this world,
And we in herds thy game, I give thee thanks . . .

It is a horrible picture of the power of love, and no reference whatsoever is made to the change supposed to be wrought in Ferdinand,
Florizel, Perdita and Miranda by love. We are in a quite different
world.

The misery which the goddess inflicts on all is well shown in the
sub-plot of the gaoler's daughter. She falls in love with Palamon,
who is never aware of the passion, and the suffering, which he is
causing. She eventually goes mad, her mind filled with images of
sexual pleasure, and in the end she is brought towards a cure by a
former suitor pretending that *he* is Palamon and going to bed with
her.

It is of the nature of desire, the play holds, that not only does it
debase and deform those it enslaves, but it can only propose a
relationship in which *person* does not very much matter. In the
relations of innocence, the *person* is everything. The gaoler's
daughter can accept a substitute[66] – and so can Emilia. With
Flavina, love was a spontaneous impulse of two children one
towards another: 'Loved for we did'; but now Emilia is 'guiltless
of election':

> This is my last
> Of vestal office: I'm bride-habited
> But maiden-hearted: a husband I have 'pointed
> But do not know him; out of two I should
> Choose one, and pray for his success, but I
> Am guiltless of election. (*V, i, 149–54*)

The story of Palamon, Arcite and Emilia is perhaps peculiarly
absurd: it reads much better in Chaucer: but the absurdity that
Emilia should accept Arcite because he wins a fight and then,
when Arcite is killed in an accident, should accept with equal
readiness his cousin is an absurdity required by Shakespeare to
prove the case against Venus and the poverty of the relationships
which she provides.

Chaucer's great study in human helplessness, of men finding
their own wretchedness as they 'seken faste after felicitee', must

have inspired Shakespeare to make his own pensive and deliberate
notes on the subject as Fletcher pursued his rapid and facile part
of the contract. The Shakespearian segment of *The Two Noble
Kinsmen* is extraordinarily gloomy – a word one would scarcely
use for any other play of Shakespeare's. People move in trance-
like fashion, move forward into their future as though into a fog,
yet they keep moving. Sexual desire is welcomed as the door to
happiness, and yet is known to be the break-up of something finer
left behind; even the lovers cannot conceal this in their compli-
ments:

> Emily,
> To buy you I have lost what's dearest to me,
> Save what is bought.   (*V, iii, 111–13*)

> O cousin,
> That we should things desire which do cost us
> The loss of our desire! That naught could buy
> Dear love but loss of dear love   (*V, iv, 109–12*)

Always away from an innocence they prize the more as they leave
it, men and women, Theseus, Palamon, Arcite, Hippolyta, Emilia
– and the gaoler's daughter – move forward driven by chance,
circumstance and Venus to a new stage of life which for most of
them has few rewards. For Palamon and Arcite in particular there
is a fatal division of self summed up in Palamon's description of
Venus's yoke as a wreath of roses which is heavier than lead and
which stings more than nettles. Their love for Emilia is the strongest thing in their lives yet every step taken towards achieving their
goal further disrupts the friendship which they know to be the
finest thing in their lives. They are like men enchanted, gladly
accepting what is forced on them by circumstance and by their
own natures, yet knowing that what they accept is their ruin.

Though there could be no one less like the Dark Woman of
the sonnets than Emilia, it is extraordinary how in 1613 the same
basic problem of the sonnets repeats itself in *The Two Noble Kinsmen*. The sexual relations with which the play is concerned are of
the chastest kind and as far as possible removed from the lust and
venereal disease of the last sonnets. But the absence of 'sin' really

makes things worse. In the last sonnets Shakespeare showed art failing to 'solve' the fatal division of man by which he is driven on to do what he knows corrupts him. In *The Two Noble Kinsmen*, Shakespeare, after all that he has held out in the Romances, and in tragedies like *Othello* and *Lear*, returns to the same insoluble division. Yet if we suppose that *here* is the final note, we mistake all that Shakespeare's career has told us. There is not and cannot be a final note in what is a perpetual movement between certainty and uncertainty, between doubt and confidence, trust and distrust, pessimism and hope. We ourselves have to ride the same movement, to accept that art can control and explain, to accept that it cannot, to accept the 'explanation' of *The Winter's Tale* as the truest, and then to veer forward to *The Two Noble Kinsmen* – or to *Troilus and Cressida* or to *Hamlet*.

Conclusion

To 'show his relevance', Shakespeare has sometimes been forced like the blind Samson to tread the measures of his philistine owners. It is the last indignity that the man who fought with his art to control absurdity should be put forward as the author of some montage of scenes of violent and meaningless bustle. It is odd, but we sometimes take pride in the uniqueness of our intellectual distress and physical menaces and, discovering that Shakespeare seems to have glimpsed something of what threatens us, we admit him as a child prodigy into the adult art of our age. With a little more humility we might see that the Shakespeare who, though ignorant of our own brutal forms of slaughter and terror, understood what hatred and cruelty were and could conceive the pressure of living in a universe without meaning, had that to offer us which is hard to find in our own art. He could have made no sense at all of the long-lived modern doctrine that the fidelity of art is to the disorder of the world. We don't need art to tell us of chaos; it is only too painfully obvious. If we are convinced that mindless drift is the sum of all that is, we might as well banish poetry from our society.

I have tried to show Shakespeare rejecting the more superficial patterns and consolations and trying to make a meeting ground between the conviction that there is no coherence and the equally strong conviction that there is coherence. Even in *King Lear* and *The Tempest* there is, to some extent, failure to accommodate the naked facts within the consolatory mould, but failure is inevitable. For when this accommodation is achieved we have reached Truth, and no poetry is needed in heaven. In the meantime, Shakespeare like all the greatest poets works for the pattern which rejects least. In the first chapter, I mentioned the three points of a triangle; the first, unorganized experience, the second the models of reality in art, the third the nature of things. The endeavour of all art, surely, is to shrink this triangle until it becomes a single point, experience, art and truth becoming synonymous. But in all art the triangle remains a triangle, however much its sides and size are reduced. Experience protests that art has not netted the whole, and truth remains at a shadowy distance. The three points are permanently and inevitably separated. Witnessing an art as great as Shakespeare's, we see the triangle diminish uniquely, so that time after time we feel compelled to say that it has gone; but given an artist as honest as Shakespeare we have to acknowledge with him that art can never bring off the consummation of embracing all experience and giving it the ultimate explanation. He is the king himself, the counterfeiter whom you cannot touch for coining, and his forgeries seem very necessary in a world trying expensively to live without the order of art or the idea of truth.

Notes

Chapter One

1 *Conversations of Lord Byron with the Countess of Blessington* (1834), p. 319.
2 Sidney, *Apology for Poetry*, ed. G. Shepherd (1965), pp. 100–1.
3 Bacon, *Philosophical Works*, ed. J. M. Robertson (1905), pp. 87–9, 111, 439–41.
4 There is a continuing debate on what Bacon really thought of poetry. A more sympathetic attitude is claimed for him in two important articles, by J. L. Harrison, 'Bacon's view of rhetoric, poetry, and the imagination' (*Huntington Library Quarterly*, XX, 1956–7, pp. 107–25), and by Anne Righter (in *The English Mind*, ed. H. S. Davies and G. Watson, 1964, pp. 7–29). Both Mr Harrison and Mrs Righter argue that there is little difference between Sidney and Bacon in that Bacon's words show him to believe that imagination, and therefore poetry, is a source of divine illumination not available from history or reason. Nevertheless, Mr Harrison's article contains the following sentence: 'And for the single reason that poetry was not a science, was not bound to the nature of things, Bacon, though fully appreciating its value, was prepared to leave it pretty much alone even though its face might be turned heavenward' (p. 119). For the other side of the debate, see L. C. Knights, *Explorations* (1946), pp. 92–111, and D. G. James, *The Dream of Learning* (1951), especially pp. 30–2, 77–80.
5 Stevens, 'Adagia', *Opus Posthumous* (1959), p. 176.
6 Joyce, *Portrait of the Artist as a Young Man*, ed. Anderson and Ellman (1964), pp. 212–13, but more fully in *Stephen Hero*, ed. T. Spencer (2nd edition, 1956), pp. 216–18.
7 Collingwood, *Principles of Art* (1938), pp. 68–9, 138, etc.

8 Supersession is discussed by M. Doran, *Endeavors of Art* (1954), pp. 305–6.
9 Wilde, 'The Decay of Lying', *Works*, ed. G. F. Maine (1948), p. 925.
10 See R. L. Gregory, *Eye and Brain: The Psychology of Seeing* (1966), *passim*, and D. Stafford Clark, *Psychiatry Today* (2nd edition, 1963), p. 135.
11 See Mircea Eliade, *Patterns in Comparative Religion* (English edition, 1958), pp. 31–3, and Chapter XII, 'The Morphology and Function of Myths'.
12 'Digression Concerning Madness' in *Tale of a Tub*.
13 Coleridge, 'On Poesy or Art', *Biographia Literaria*, ed. Shawcross (1907), vol. II, pp. 253–4.
14 The phrase 'festive comedy' is taken from C. L. Barber's book, *Shakespeare's Festive Comedy* (1959).
15 See for example E. C. Pettet, *Shakespeare and the Romance Tradition* (1949), N. Frye, *A Natural Perspective* (1965), S. Wells, 'Shakespeare and Romance', in *Later Shakespeare*, ed. J. R. Brown and B. Harris (1966), pp. 48–79.
16 See a learned and amusing essay by T. J. B. Spencer, 'The Sophistry of Shakespeare', *English Studies Today*, 4th Series (Rome, 1966), pp. 169–85.
17 For a note on the ending of *Henry V*, see my 'Shakespeare's Romances: 1900–1957' in *Shakespeare Survey*, 11, p. 18.

Chapter Two

18 Dowden, *Shakspere's Sonnets* (1883), p. lix.
19 See *Shakespeare 1564–1964*, ed. E. A. Bloom (1964), pp. 136–53; the thesis is supported by J. Dover Wilson in the New Cambridge Shakespeare edition of the sonnets (1966), pp. xxviii and 242–4.
20 Auden, introduction to the Signet edition of the sonnets (1964), p. xxxv.
21 See the discussion by W. A. Ringler, *Poems of Sir Philip Sidney* (1962), p. 423.
22 Auden, *op. cit.*, pp. xxxvii–xxxviii.

Chapter Three

23 See the New Arden edition by R. A. Foakes, p. 106, and C. J. Sisson, *New Readings in Shakespeare* (1956), vol. I, pp. 97–8.

24 Compare B. Roesen (*sc.* A. Righter), '*Love's Labour's Lost*', *Shakespeare Quarterly*, IV (1953), p. 412.

Chapter Four

25 Frye, *A Natural Perspective*, p. 101; other quotations are from pp. 92, 100, 103–4.
26 *Modern Language Review*, LVI (1961), 248–9.
27 For a different view of Theseus and the play-within-the-play, see J. R. Brown, *Shakespeare and his Comedies* (1957), pp. 87–90.
28 The phrase is used by E. W. Talbert in *Elizabethan Drama and Shakespeare's Early Plays* (1963), p. 73. See also my *Thomas Kyd and Early Elizabethan Tragedy* (1966), pp. 32–3.
29 *Shakespeare's World of Images* (1949), chapter 3.
30 *Homo Ludens* (English edition, 1949), p. 14.

Chapter Five

31 *Johnson on Shakespeare*, ed. Ralegh (1908), pp. 28, 16, 15.
32 See G. Bullough, *Narrative and Dramatic Sources of Shakespeare*, vol. I (1957), pp. 269–83.

Chapter Six

33 I am thinking particularly of Kott's *Shakespeare Our Contemporary* and productions by the Royal Shakespeare Company apparently influenced by Kott's work.
34 Arnold, Preface to *Poems*, 1853; see *Poems*, ed. K. Allott (1965), p. 591.
35 *How Shakespeare Spent the Day* (1963), p. 72.
36 *The Question of Hamlet* (1959), p. 106.
37 For a full discussion of this view of *The Spanish Tragedy*, see my *Thomas Kyd and Early Elizabethan Tragedy* (1966).
38 For a brief review of the multitudinous interpretations, see E. M. W. Tillyard, *Shakespeare's Problem Plays* (1950), pp. 146–9.
39 Letters, ed. Wade (1954), p. 741.
40 See, for example, R. W. Battenhouse, *Shakespeare Studies I* (ed. Barroll, 1965), pp. 357–8, and L. C. Knights, *An Approach to Hamlet* (1960).

Chapter Seven

41 See, for example, P. Ure, *Shakespeare: The Problem Plays* (1961), p. 38, and Frye, *A Natural Perspective*, p. 42.

42 *The Ulysses Theme* (2nd edition, 1963), pp. 167–8.
43 *Utopia*, ed. Arber (1869), pp. 64–6; ed. Collins (1904), pp. 40–2.

Chapter Eight

44 Tillyard, *Shakespeare's Problem Plays* (1950), pp. 104–6; Hunter, introduction to the New Arden edition (1959), pp. xxxvi–xxxvii.
45 Tillyard, *Shakespeare's Problem Plays*, p. 116.
46 See A. P. Rossiter's admirable comments on the play in *Angel With Horns* (1961), especially p. 125.

Chapter Nine

47 *Three Plays for Puritans* (standard edition, 1931), pp. xxvii–xxviii.
48 J. K. Walton, in 'Lear's Last Speech' (*Shakespeare Survey* 13, 1960, pp. 11–19) argues against the generally accepted view that Lear supposes Cordelia to be still alive.
49 *The Wheel of Fire* (1930), edition of 1960, pp. 174, 204.
50 M. C. Bradbrook's original approach to the form of the play in *The Tragic Pageant of 'Timon of Athens'* (1966) leads to very different conclusions about the play's condition.
51 'Symbolism of Poetry', reprinted in *Essays and Introductions* (1961), p. 156. See also 'The Irish Dramatic Movement' (1904), reprinted in *Explorations* (1962), p. 163.
52 *Statesman's Manual* (1817), quoted by Shawcross in his edition of *Biographia Literaria* (1907), p. lxxiii.

Chapter Ten

53 See my 'Shakespeare's Romances: 1900–1957' (*Shakespeare Survey* 11, 1958), pp. 1–18.
54 This was the tentative conclusion of my study, 'An Approach to the Problem of *Pericles*' (*Shakespeare Survey* 5, 1952), pp. 25–49.
55 In the text as we have it, Lysimachus says that he was only pretending to try Marina's virtue, but there is strong evidence that the compiler of the text misinterpreted the scene. See the article cited in the previous note, pp. 41–4.
56 *The John Fletcher Plays* (1962), pp. 148–9, and *Shakespeare's Tragedies* (1950), Chapter 7.
57 See J. H. P. Pafford's note to IV, iii, 37 in the New Arden edition.
58 In the Signet edition of *The Winter's Tale*, E. Schanzer puts a different interpretation on Perdita's words and thereby challenges

the notion that 'the year growing ancient' refers to the timing of the feast.

59 For the neoplatonic views of Venus, see E. Panofsky, *Studies in Iconology* (edition of 1962), pp. 142–5.

60 *The Approach to Shakespeare* (1930), p. 106.

61 See the discussion by A. Righter, *Shakespeare and the Idea of the Play* (1962), pp. 202–3.

62 *On the Boiler* (1938), p. 22.

63 It has been maintained that Shakespeare alone was responsible for *Henry VIII*. I remember hearing F. S. Boas, then a very old man, saying he would go to the stake to maintain that Fletcher shared the writing. I should like to have the courage to follow him.

64 An extended version of these remarks on *The Two Noble Kinsmen* will be found in *Review of English Literature*, October 1964.

65 'dividual': the quarto reads 'individual'.

66 I am indebted here to the excellent discussion by Leech in *The John Fletcher Plays*.

Index

Allott, K., 165
Amis, Kingsley, 8
Apollonius of Tyre, 140
Ariosto, Ludovico, 36
Arnold, Matthew, 84, 165
Auden, W. H., 18, 30, 164
Austen, Jane, 11

Bacon, Francis, 1, 2, 9, 15, 53, 55, 153, 163
Balzac, Honoré de, 11
Barber, C. L., 34, 47, 49–50, 51–2, 53, 56, 65, 164
Battenhouse, R. W., 165
Blackfriars, 153
Blackmur, R. P., 19
Blessington, Countess of, 163
Bloom, E. A., 164
Boas, F. S., 167
Bradbrook, M. C., 166
Brook, Peter, 43
Brooke, Arthur, 77
Brown, Ivor, 84
Brown, J. R., 165
Bullough, G., 165
Burbage, R., 84, 91
Bush, D., 27
Byron, George Gordon, 1, 163

Chamberlain's Men, Lord, 84
Chambers, E. K., 71
Chaucer, Geoffrey, 157
Clark, D. Stafford, 164
Coleridge, S. T., 9–10, 164
Collingwood, R. G., 4–5, 163

Conrad, Joseph, 9
Victory, 142
Cruttwell, Patrick, 19

Defoe, Daniel
Robinson Crusoe, 142
Dickens, Charles, 11
Doran, M., 164
Dowden, Edward, 17, 164

Eliade, M., 69, 164
Eliot, T. S., 31
Ellis-Fermor, Una, 96
Ellman, R., 163

Fiedler, Leslie, 19
Fletcher, John, 153, 167
Foakes, R. A., 164
Frye, Northrop, 19, 33, 49, 50–1, 62, 70, 164, 165

Golding, William
Lord of the Flies, 142
Gregory, R. L., 164

Hall, Edward, 84
Harbage, A., 27
Hardy, Thomas, 11
Harrison, J. L., 163
Hobbes, Thomas, 106
Holinshed, R., 84
Hooker, Richard, 106
Hubler, E., 19
Huizinga, J., 69
Hunter, G. K., 110, 113–4, 166

Ingram, W. G., 27

James, D. G., 163
Johnson, Samuel, 10, 73
Jonson, Ben, 139
    Bartholomew Fair, 101
Joyce, James, 4, 163

Knight, Wilson, 19, 132, 138
Knights, L. C., 163, 165
Krieger, Murray, 19
Kyd, Thomas,
    The Spanish Tragedy, 56, 71, 80,
        84–6, 87, 92

Lamb, Mary, 116
Landry, C. H., 19
Lawrence, D. H.,
    The Man Who Loved Islands, 142
Leech, Clifford, 146, 167

Mackail, J. W., 151
Maine, G. F., 164
Middleton, Thomas, 134
Milton, John,
    Il Penseroso, 37
More, Thomas
    Utopia, 103, 142
Morley, Thomas, 63

O'Casey, Sean, 91

Pafford, J. H. P., 166
Panofsky, E., 167
Pettet, E. C., 164
Pickering, John,
    Horestes, 86
Plato, 1, 3, 9
Porto, Luigi da, 77

Redpath, T., 27
Righter, Ann (Roesen, B.), 48, 163,
    165, 167
Ringler, W. A., 164
Robertson, J. M., 163
Roesen, B., *see* Righter, Ann
Rossiter, A. P., 166

Schanzer, E., 166

Shakespeare, William,
    Sonnets, The, **17–31**, 37, 51,
        106, 132, 158–9
    All's Well That Ends Well, 11,
        14, 34, 71, 95, 108, **109–115,**
        119, 123, 129, 133, 144
    Antony and Cleopatra, 5, 6, 11,
        14, **121–2,** 133
    As You Like It, 5, 10, 11, 34,
        35, 40, 49, **56–63,** 65, 71, 84,
        108, 128, 131, 142
    Comedy of Errors, 10, 11, 12,
        33–4, 35, 69, 142
    Coriolanus, 121, 133
    Cymbeline, 12, 132, 139, 144,
        154
    Hamlet, 11, 81, **83–93,** 95, 96,
        101, 123, 144, 159
    Henry IV, pts. 1 & 2; 5, 71
    Henry V, 14, 108, 164
    Henry VIII, 153
    Julius Caesar, 10, 83
    King Lear, 5, 11, 15, 95, 121,
        122, **128–33,** 135, 138, 143,
        159, 161
    Love's Labour's Lost, 10, 13, 27,
        37–48, 62, 71, 76, 131, 143
    Macbeth, 11, 83, 121, **122–3,** 127
    Measure for Measure, 12, 30, 34,
        36, 71, 73, 95, 108, 109–10,
        114, **115–19,** 123, 129, 133,
        144, 150
    Merchant of Venice, The, 12, 71,
        109, 116
    Merry Wives of Windsor, 71, 95
    Midsummer Night's Dream, 3, 11,
        13, 34, 49, **51–6,** 62, 66, 71,
        73, 84, 135
    Much Ado About Nothing, 34,
        35, 71, 109
    Othello, 5, 11, 12, 15, 91, 95,
        108, 121, 122, **123–8,** 144,
        159
    Pericles, 12, 30, 37, 69, 132, 136,
        138, **139–41,** 142, 146, 153–4
    Richard II, 5, 6, 72, 83
    Richard III, 72, 83
    Romeo and Juliet, 48, 53, **71–81,**
        90, 91, 101, 131

Shakespeare, William—contd.
   Taming of the Shrew, 10, 36
   Tempest, The, 5, 6, 12, 13, 14,
      30, 36, 69, 73, 119, 132, 138,
      139, 142–3, 144, **150–3**, 154,
      161
   Timon of Athens, 121, **133–8**
   Troilus and Cressida, 11, 14, 60,
      91, 95, **96–108**, 110, 123, 127,
      133, 144, 159
   Twelfth Night, 3, 10, 11, 12, 14,
      34, 35, 49, 56, **63–9**, 71,
      95
   Two Gentlemen of Verona, 10,
      34, 35
   Two Noble Kinsmen, The, 30,
      146, 153, **154–9**
   Winter's Tale, The, 12, 30, 35,
      37, 60, 132, 139, **141–50**, 154,
      159
Shawcross, J., 164, 166
Shepherd, G., 163
Sidney, Philip, 1, 2, 7, 10, 15, 18,
   54, 163
Sisson, C. J., 164
Spanish Tragedy, The, see Kyd,
   Thomas
Spencer, T., 163
Spencer, T. J. B., 164

Stanford, W. B., 101
Stauffer, D. A., 67
Stevens, Wallace, 4, 163
Stirling, Brents, 17, 22, 31
Swift, Jonathan, 8–9
   Gulliver's Travels, 142
Synge, J. M.,
   Riders to the Sea, 142

Talbert, E. W., 165
Tillyard, E. M. W., 110, 113, 165,
   166
Tolstoy, Leo, 3

Ure, P., 165

Venus, 151, 156, 157, 167
Vico, G. B., 152

Walton, J. K., 166
Weiss, Peter, 85
Wells, S., 164
Wilde, Oscar, 3, 8, 164
Wilson, J. Dover, 164
Wordsworth, William, 95

Yeats, W. B., 9, 10, 19, 91, 135–6,
   152